IMPROVISING EARLY MUSIC

*This eleventh publication in the series
"Collected Writings of the Orpheus Institute"
is edited by Dirk Moelants*

IMPROVISING EARLY MUSIC

The History of Musical Improvisation
from the Late Middle Ages
to the Early Baroque

Rob C. Wegman
Johannes Menke
Peter Schubert

COLLECTED WRITINGS OF THE
ORPHEUS
INSTITUTE

Leuven University Press
2014

CONTENTS

PREFACE / P. 7

— Rob C. Wegman
What is counterpoint? / P. 9

— Johannes Menke
"Ex centro" improvisation - Sketches for a theory of sound progressions in the early baroque / P. 69

— Peter Schubert
From improvisation to composition: three 16th century case studies / P. 93

PERSONALIA / P. 131

COLOPHON / P. 135

PREFACE

The study of improvised music is always a challenge, due to its volatility and unpredictability. But what about studying musical improvisation from before the age of sound recordings? In this book three experts give their view on aspects of musical improvisation in the late medieval, renaissance and early baroque periods. In his contribution, Rob Wegman surprisingly starts from the story of Beethoven's lessons with Haydn to lead us all the way back to the 14th century and the origins of counterpoint. From there he takes up the history of improvised counterpoint, searching for traces of this practice in written sources. Seemingly a somewhat frustrating search, as it seems impossible to get full access to the experience of improvised counterpoint, but in his search, the author finds clear traces of improvisation in written music.

The main topic of the paper by Johannes Menke is musical practice in the 16th and the 17th centuries, focussing not so much on the revolutionary changes that mark the transition to the Baroque period, but on those aspects of composition and improvisation that do not change radically. The central concept here is 'ex centro' sound structure: the practice of writing or improvising a soprano over a bass, rather than working around a central tenor. Although this practice is often considered as a feature of the Baroque, Menke traces this practice all the way back to the 15th century.

The paper by Peter Schubert, finally, gives a more practical approach. Starting from an overview of improvisation techniques found in treatises from the Renaissance period, he gives examples, both from written compositions and from his own personal improvisation practice, to illustrate them and to make the link between improvisation and techniques used by composers in the 16th century.

As a whole, this volume shows us through historical sources how improvisation was an integral part of music education and how closely improvisation and composition were linked. This gives new insights in the way music was performed in its original historical context and a new way to look at written scores from the past.

Dirk Moelants

WHAT IS COUNTERPOINT?
Rob C. Wegman

I.

I would like to begin this contribution by taking the reader back to a year in the life of Ludwig van Beethoven. The year is 1792, and in that year, Beethoven was a young man in his early twenties. Although he was not well known outside his native city of Bonn, where he lived and worked, he had already been making a name for himself as an exceptionally talented musician and composer. Yet for a man of his promise a provincial town like Bonn was clearly too confining a place. It lacked the sorts of opportunities he would need to realize his artistic gifts and aspirations. To everybody who knew the young Beethoven, it was obvious that he should go to the musical capital of the world—to Vienna, the city of Mozart and Haydn. It is true that Mozart had died the previous year. Yet the aging Haydn was still there, and was known to give private tuition to paying students.

Few pupils could have seemed more deserving of study with Haydn than Beethoven. Earlier that year, Ludwig had briefly met the older composer, and had shown him some of his recent compositions. To gain an impression of what he was able to show Haydn on that day, I would recommend listening to his Cantata on the Death of Emperor Joseph II of 1790 (WoO 87), an ambitious setting for soloists, orchestra, and choir, altogether lasting about 40 minutes, that richly testifies to the young man's technical assurance as well as to his ability to summon the dramatic power of the Viennese classical language.[1]

---

1. Among available recordings of this fine Cantata (of which unfortunately there are not many), I would recommend the one recorded in 1970 by the BBC Symphony Orchestra with BBC Chorus and Choral Society, dir. Sir Colin Davis, featuring Kiri Te Kanawa, soprano; Yvonne Newman, alto; David Barrett, tenor; and Michael Langdon, bass.

If Beethoven was able to write music of such accomplishment around the age of twenty, one might justifiably wonder how much he actually stood learn from Haydn, indeed whether he needed any lessons at all. Yet his friends in Bonn were not concerned about this. They felt that Haydn could give him something vastly more important than compositional skill alone. As one of those friends said on the eve of Beethoven's departure, "With the help of assiduous labor you shall receive Mozart's spirit from Haydn's hands."

It was a beautiful prophecy, but one that would come true only in part—and unfortunately it was not the part about Mozart's spirit, but rather the one about assiduous labor. Within a week of his arrival in Vienna, Beethoven started taking lessons with Haydn. Yet these were not lessons in advanced composition. Haydn was not giving him expert guidance on how to put together a string quartet, or how to write a symphony, or a concerto. Instead, Beethoven received instruction in that most basic and elementary of subjects in music: the theory of counterpoint.[2]

We still have a fair idea of what took place in these early lessons, for Beethoven never discarded his old counterpoint exercises, and they survive today in libraries around the world. It is apparent from these exercises that Haydn followed the pedagogy set forth in the influential textbook *Gradus ad Parnassum* (1725) of Johann Joseph Fux—a book from which Haydn himself had once learned the art through arduous self-study. Like so many textbooks in this period, *Gradus ad Parnassum* was set up as a dialogue between Joseph, a youthful, eager student, and Aloys, a firm but kindly master:[3]

> ALOYS. Let us settle down to work, then, and make a beginning in the name of Almighty God, the fountain of all wisdom.

---

2. For this and what follows, see Alfred Mann, "Beethoven's Contrapuntal Studies With Haydn," in: *Musical Quarterly* 56 (1970): 711–26.; see also Ignatius von Seyfried, *Louis van Beethoven's Studies in Thorough-Bass, Counterpoint and the Art of Scientific Composition*, trans. Henry Hugh Pierson, (Leipzig: Schuberth, 1853).
3. Cited after Johann Joseph Fux, *The Study of Counterpoint from Johann Joseph Fux's* Gradus ad Parnassum, trans. Alfred Mann (New York: Morton, 1943), 22.

What is Counterpoint?

JOSEPH. Before we start on the exercises, revered master, may I still ask what one is to understand by the term *counterpoint*? I have heard this word used not only by musicians but also by laymen.

ALOYS. Your question is a good one, for this is to be the first subject of our study and work. It is necessary for you to know that in earlier times, instead of our modern notes, dots, or points were used. Thus one used to call a composition in which point was set against, or counter, to point, *counterpoint*; this usage is still followed today, even though the form of the notes has been changed. By the term counterpoint therefore is understood a composition which is written strictly according to technical rules. The study of counterpoint comprises several species which we shall consider in turn. First of all, then, the simplest species.

The simplest species: this was to be the starting point for Beethoven, too. In the first lesson, Haydn played him a tune in whole notes on the piano, told him that it was known as the *cantus firmus*, and then explained how to write a counter-melody, also in whole notes—conceived, literally, as point against point. That, he said, was the first species of counterpoint. This was to be followed, in a rigorous and methodical curriculum, by the second species—writing two notes against one. Finally he gave Beethoven some exercises to complete at home.

If one could play through some of those exercises, which actually still survive, it would be hard to believe one's ears. Did Beethoven really have to travel all the way from Bonn to be given such childishly simple homework? Was this the sort of work that would allow him to make the best of the opportunity to study with Haydn? Even if there had been a genuine deficiency in his musical training, surely there were plenty of musicians back in Bonn who could have taught him stuff like this? And if we recall that early cantata on the death of Emperor Leopold, which showed such considerable accomplishment in the art of composition, was it not rather demeaning for Beethoven to arrive in Vienna only to be sent back, as it were, to grade school?

As it turns out Beethoven was not very happy about Haydn's teaching, and he soon decided that he would make more progress if he took additional lessons from another Viennese composer, Johann Georg Albrechtsberger. Yet it was not the counterpoint that was the problem. Beethoven must have really valued the lessons, otherwise he would surely not have held on to his exercise books, with all his errors and Haydn's corrections, for the rest of his life. Nor would he have approached Albrechtsberger for additional instruction in counterpoint. The real reason, it seems, is that Haydn and Beethoven did not get along especially well. The older man soon appears to have lost interest in his new pupil, and Beethoven—who had always been laboring under Mozart's shadow—felt injured by the apparent rejection.

So, yes, Beethoven was quite willing, even at age twenty-one, to submit to this tedious course of studies, even under a less than enthusiastic teacher, in order to acquire the art of counterpoint. He did not experience that as demeaning at all. So what was the value he perceived in these lessons? What did counterpoint represent to him? What, in his view, had been lacking in the compositions he had already written before his departure to Vienna? And how did he expect his training in counterpoint to improve them?

When dealing with questions such as these, writers often invoke an analogy with language. That is to say, if the art of composition can be seen as a kind of language, then the rules of counterpoint would be its grammar. The analogy makes a certain kind of sense. We can all learn a language by speaking along with native speakers, and after a while we may even become quite fluent in it—this, of course, is how we learned our mother tongue. Yet without formal training in the grammar and syntax of language, in the underlying structure, we may never feel totally confident that we have truly mastered it. If we were to publish prose compositions in that language, we might always be afraid that sooner or later somebody would spot an embarrassing grammatical error, one that would give away our lack of training. So we might well feel, even at age twenty, that it could be useful to receive a thorough grounding in grammar before moving on, say, to advanced creative writing.

Maybe this is how we could view the case of Beethoven. His lessons in counterpoint may have been mindlessly boring, like exercises in the declension of Latin verbs, yet the pedagogy would also instil in him a certain discipline, would lay a technical foundation that would support his more advanced artistic endeavors.

What is Counterpoint?

And yet there is something contradictory in all of this. To judge from his early compositions, Beethoven seems to have been a perfectly competent composer even without training in counterpoint. And if that is true, then how indispensible a foundation was counterpoint really? Was it actually a foundation—in the sense that it must be completed before one can construct the actual building? To return to our analogy with language, is it not true that by the time we are taught the grammar of our native tongue—in my case, in school around the age of eight—we are already fluent speakers, and do not actually need the grammar to make ourselves understood? Is grammar not really an afterthought, a distillation of rules and principles that naturally evolved in living language, well before it occurred to anyone to write them down?

With this last question, we are already touching on the theme I propose to explore in this contribution—the question of improvisation. When it comes to language, we are all improvisers, we literally improvise all day long. In everyday speech, we utter the first words of a sentence even before we know how that sentence is going to end. By the time we have completed the sentence, it always turns out as a perfectly formed syntactic whole, neatly obeying the rules of grammar—even though we have given those rules scarcely any thought while uttering it. The same is true of discourse at large. When we speak, we do not always know what we are going to say a minute from now, or how we are going to say it. All we know is that we will say whatever seems appropriate at that point, and we are not going to worry about it until we get there.

Maybe this is where the analogy between counterpoint and grammar breaks down. While it may be true that the counterpoint lessons gave Beethoven a kind of musical grammar, it certainly was not the grammar of a living language. By the eighteenth century, counterpoint was a dead language, no longer spoken, no longer evolving. It was a set of abstract theory exercises on paper, useful perhaps from a pedagogical point of view, yet for professional musicians it was perfectly possible to get by without formal training in it—as Beethoven's early compositions amply demonstrate.

Once upon a time, of course, it had been different—counterpoint had been a living language.[4] Long before Beethoven's time, mastering counterpoint had meant more, much more, than the ability to write exercises. It had meant being able to sing it on the spot, in exactly the same way that you and I speak language on the spot. It meant to sing music that observed the rules of counterpoint as naturally and self-evidently as our everyday sentences obey the rules of grammar. Doing so may not have been called "improvisation" at the time, but then we do not call our everyday speech "improvisation" either—even though technically it is just that. It was called "to sing counterpoint," or just "to sing," just as we talk about speaking language, or just speaking.

This is the state of affairs as it must have prevailed in the fifteenth and sixteenth centuries. People learned counterpoint by doing it, and many must have acquired it simply by singing along, picking up the idiom just as we are likely to pick up a language if we stay in another country for long enough. So perhaps this is how we might view the question raised earlier. Why did Beethoven still need to learn the grammar of counterpoint in his early twenties? Because for him, counterpoint was a dead language, because he had never had the chance to speak that language in its pure form. For that very reason, it did not really matter that he learned counterpoint so late in life, and in so academic a fashion. After all, he would never be required to speak it as a living language.

In the Renaissance, on the other hand, the situation had been very different. Consider what Johannes Tinctoris wrote in the last chapter of his treatise on counterpoint, the *Liber de arte contrapuncti* of 1477. "I have known not even one man," he says, "who has achieved eminent or noble rank among musicians if he began to compose or to sing *super librum* [that is, to improvise counterpoint] at or above his twentieth year of age."[5] So by

---

4. For this and what follows, see Rob C. Wegman, "From Maker to Composer: Improvisation and Musical Authorship in the Low Countries, 1450–1500," *Journal of the American Musicological Society* 49 (1996): 409–79.
5. After Johannes Tinctoris, *The Art of Counterpoint* (Liber de arte contrapuncti), trans. Albert Seay, Musicological Studies and Documents 5 (American Institute of Musicology, 1961), 141.

fifteenth-century standards, Beethoven might as well have given up any hope of ever becoming a musician of any competence. A living language—which counterpoint for Tinctoris certainly was—has to be acquired in childhood, otherwise it will be too late. Here the analogy with language works very well indeed. For if a child has not learned to speak any language by the age of about eight, then he or she never will learn to speak, because the brain can only develop the wiring for speech during a circumscribed phase of its early development. After that, the opportunity will be gone forever.

In order to acquire counterpoint as a living language, the kind of curriculum that Beethoven endured in Vienna would have been of little value. It is not through written exercises that we learn to speak a language, but rather by actively speaking it. A fifteenth-century choirboy had to sing and practice counterpoint, day after day, learn from his mistakes, listen to how others were doing it, follow their example, until he had internalized the language, and could handle it as effortlessly as you or I can conduct a conversation on the phone. That may seem like a lot to demand from a child. On the other hand, counterpoint was the only music, apart from plainchant, that anyone was ever likely to hear. In the fifteenth and sixteenth centuries, counterpoint was the world language in music, the musical *lingua franca* spoken everywhere in Western Europe, from England to Denmark, to Poland and Bohemia, to Spain and Italy—and, in the sixteenth century, even in the new world. What was not counterpoint or plainchant had no claim to being music at all.

At some point in its history, then, counterpoint must have died, passed from the living language it had been in the Renaissance, to the dead language that Beethoven was at such considerable pains to learn. The likely cause of death is not hard to guess. The fatal blow to counterpoint probably came around 1600, with the identification of a new musical style. That style that had grown out of counterpoint, and still needed counterpoint for a reference, but at the same time permitted, even encouraged, violations of contrapuntal rules for the sake of rhetorical effect. Once this new style, the *seconda pratica*, was in place, any musical innovation driven by rhetorical concerns was bound to be introduced only in this style, which as a consequence would undergo dramatic development. The old style, counterpoint proper, was now referred to as the *prima pratica*. Fairly soon, theorists began to insist that the distinction between these two styles be kept neat and tidy, and so they discouraged stylistic experimentation in the older style.[6] It was the job of counterpoint to stay put, and never to develop beyond the specific idiom it had acquired by the late sixteenth century. We can see this as early as 1610, when Claudio Monteverdi published his *Missa In illo tempore*. In this work, an exercise in the *prima pratica*, the art of counterpoint seems to want to dwell forever in a bygone age, oblivious to anything going on in the contemporary worlds of opera, madrigal, and oratorio.

As a relic from an increasingly remote past, the *stile antico* (as counterpoint came to be called in the seventeenth century) would soon acquire an aura of venerable antiquity; indeed it became the very byword of authority and tradition.[7] We like to think of composers like Bach and Beethoven as returning to that tradition in old age, re-engaging with ever more uncompromisingly abstract forms of counterpoint, as if appreciating, like never before, the true depth and value of this ancient art. Undoubtedly it was this aura of antiquity and authority, this promise of hidden riches and depth, that motivated the young Beethoven to keep going with his exercises. He may not have received Mozart's spirit from Haydn's hands, but at least he was drinking from the same fountain that had once lavished that spirit. And one day, surely, it would lavish his own.

---

6. Cf. Lorenzo Bianconi, *Music in the Seventeenth Century*, trans. David Bryant (Cambridge: Cambridge University Press, 1987), 47–48: in 1643 Marco Scacchi raised strong objections against the mixing of elements from both the *prima* and *seconda pratica*, especially in works belonging to the former category, that is, old-style vocal counterpoint. The result, Bianconi notes, is that Scacchi's classicism "defines, codifies and consolidates the position of an 'ancient' *a cappella* style of Counter-Reformation polyphony in a way *that sets it apart from all notion of historical change*; it can, indeed, appear alongside – though *not together with* – other more modern styles when required by the text, occasion or destination of the work in question" (my italics).

7. Cf. Christoph Wolff, *Der stile antico in der Music Johann Sebastian Bachs: Studien zu Bachs Spätwerk*, Beihefte zum Archiv für Musikwissenschaft 6 (Wiesbaden: Steiner, 1968).

2.

It may be helpful to think of the history of counterpoint as being marked by this major break around 1600. Yet the break is not quite so clear-cut as I have made it sound; there is also a great deal of continuity. While there is no question that counterpoint was the language in which polyphony was improvised during the fifteenth and sixteenth centuries, it was of course also the language of composition. The written dimension was there from the very beginning. The difference is that for Beethoven the only access to counterpoint was through writing; had he lived three centuries earlier, he would already have learned it in childhood, by listening and singing no less than by reading and writing.

There are other continuities that are perhaps less obvious, and one of my aims here is to explore what they are. To do this, we are now going to leap back five centuries, from Beethoven's time to the decades around the year 1300—the time in history that counterpoint, so far as we can tell, made its first entry on the European musical scene. My question is going to be a simple one, and it is about continuity: when counterpoint first emerges, what is new and distinctive about the art, and which of those new and distinctive things can still be recognized in the counterpoint that Beethoven learned several centuries later? If we can answer these questions, then perhaps we can also understand why and how this medieval practice could have had such a lasting impact on Western music history, to the point where we are still taking counterpoint lessons today. In this respect counterpoint could be compared to the mechanical clock or the pipe organ, two other inventions from around 1300 that have transformed the course of Western history forever.

Let us quickly review the evidence that has been brought together by other scholars, especially by the world expert on counterpoint, Klaus-Jürgen Sachs, on whose work I rely in what follows.[8] To begin with, one of the really odd things about

---

8. For this and what follows, see Klaus-Jürgen Sachs, *Der Contrapunctus im 14. und 15. Jahrhundert: Untersuchungen zum Terminus, zur Lehre u. zu den Quellen*, Beiheft zum Archiv für Musikwissenschaft 13 (Wiesbaden: Steiner, 1974).

counterpoint is how suddenly it emerges, and how suddenly every writer seems to agree on its central importance. The decade in which it first turns up is the 1330s. There is one music treatise from that decade whose author clearly knows what counterpoint is, and who provides rules on how to make it.[9] In fact it is dated precisely in 1336. The author is a monk in Picardy named Pierre Palmoiseuse or, as he names himself in Latin, Petrus dictus Palma ociosa. He lives in a monastery in the diocese of Amiens, a monastery that belongs to the Cistercian order—not one of the orders that we would ordinarily associate with the cultivation of polyphony, for its guiding principle, if anything, was austerity. But maybe there is a clue in there somehow.

Now Petrus, as soon as he is past the opening preamble of his treatise, begins to talk directly about a kind of polyphony that we have not encountered in any treatise before him. He does not call it counterpoint quite yet, but rather speaks of *simplex discantus*, a term we have not come across before either.

> Unde notandum est, quod omnis **simplex discantus**, qui nihil aliud est quam **punctus contra punctum sive notula naturalibus instrumentis formata contra aliam notulam**, simpliciter potest componi et ordinari ex unisono, semiditono, ditono, diapente, tono cum diapente et diapason.
>
> It is to be noted that all **plain discant**—which is nothing other than **point against point, or one note produced on natural instruments against another note**—can be put together and arranged simply from unison, minor third, major third, fifth, sixth, and octave.

Let us briefly consider those two words. *Discantus*, at this time, is more or less the catch-all term for polyphony. So what must be distinctive about the particular type he discusses is that it is *simplex*. Now the literal meaning of *simplex* is not "simple" in the sense of "easy to understand," that is, the opposite of complicated, but rather: one-fold, or undivided—a meaning still

---

9. Only available edition to date: Johannes Wolf, "Ein Beitrag zur Diskantlehre des 14. Jahrhunderts," *Sammelbände der Internationalen Musikgesellschaft* 15 (1913–14): 505-34.

retained in the German word for simple, *einfach*, as opposed to *zweifach*, or *dreifach*. If a Euro coin could be said to be *simplex*, then a ten-cent piece represents part of a Euro that is no longer *simplex*, because it has been broken up in pieces like this. A Euro made up by smaller coins is *multiplex*.

Yet how can discant be *simplex*, one-fold, when it is polyphony and thus by definition consisting of two or more voices? The answer is that Petrus is not talking about the number of voices, but about the quality of the notes. Like those Euro coins, those notes have to be kept whole: Petrus is not going to deal in small change. *Discantus simplex* consists only of whole notes, notes that are not broken up into smaller rhythmic values. And those whole notes are notated in neumes, the plainchant notation in which there is no specification of rhythmic value. What he is saying, in effect, is that this is polyphony without rhythm. It moves only in notes that have no specific durational value, that are whole and unbroken. Apparently not every reader was expected to grasp this immediately, for Petrus went on to spell it out more clearly. *Simplex discantus*, he goes on to say in the passage cited above, "is nothing other than point against point, or one note produced on natural instruments against another note."

This is the first time in the history of music theory that we encounter the fateful concept of *punctus contra punctum*. Or perhaps it is better to put it differently: this is the first time that we encounter the expression. For the concept of singing one note against another is of course as old as Western polyphony itself, and indeed was still being perpetuated around this time in the so-called *Klangschrittlehre*. A new expression, then, for what appears to have been a very old practice. As chance would have it, this same expression turns up in another context not too long before the writing of Petrus de Palma ociosa's treatise. This is a poem by the troubadour Peire de Corbiac, entitled *Trézor*, and written in southern France around the middle of the thirteenth century. In it, the poet boasts of his many musical skills, and his ability to apply them both in church and in society at large. "Now, Lords" he says,[10]

> Senhors, encar sai ieu molt devinablamenz,
> chantar en sancta glieiza per ponz e per asenz,
> choris *sanctus* et *agnus* tripar contipotens,
> entonar *seculorum* que nol faill us *amens*,
> e far dous chantz et orgues e contrapointamens.
> Ja sai chansons enotas e vers bos e valens,
> pastorelas apres amorozas, plazens,
> retroenchas e dansas, ben e cortesamens.
> De totas res del segle sai aver grazimens,
> de clercs, de cavaliers, de dompnas avinens,
> de borçes, de joglars, d'escudiers, de servens.

> ... I know very resourcefully indeed
> How to sing in Holy Church by points and by accents,
> Dance the Sanctus and Agnus and Cunctipotens,
> Intone *seculorum* followed without fail by *amen*,
> And make sweet chants and organa and counterpoints.
> Indeed I know notated songs, and good and worthy verses,
> I have learned *pastorelas*, lovely and pleasing,
> *Retroenchas* and *dansas*, noble and courtly.
> Of all things of the world I know how to have the favor
> Of clerics, knights, and honorable ladies,
> Of burghers, *joglars*, students, and servants.

Contrapointamens: it is the first time that the word "counterpoint" turns up outside the realm of music theory. The particular line of Peire's poem that contains the word is not found in all manuscript copies: the few copies that have it, however, all date from the early fourteenth century, and are thus roughly contemporary with the treatise of Petrus de Palma ociosa. So while the practice of singing note-against-note polyphony was not exactly a novelty, it does seem to have called for a new technical designation by the

---

10. After Elizabeth Aubrey, "References to Music in Old Occitan Literature," *Acta Musicologica* 61 (1989): 110–49, at 147–48.

early fourteenth century. And it so happens that this designation was to become virtually synonymous with "good music" for centuries to come.

As a music historian I have always been fascinated by the question when, where, and why certain keywords in the understanding or appreciation of music appear or disappear. For such changes are almost invariably indicative of broader shifts in thinking about music. I would argue that this is true even of the word "counterpoint," despite the fact that note-against-note singing in itself was not a novelty at all. The give-away in a new word or concept is usually an implied opposition to something else. You can tell this from my own attempt, a moment ago, to explain the words of Petrus de Palma ociosa. Why does he speak of *cantus simplex*? Answer: because it is not *cantus multiplex*. Instead of the small change of semibreves and minims, which the reader apparently knows already, he wants us to think of whole coins, unbroken and unmeasured. True, we are still talking about the same old practice of note-against-note singing. But *simplex* is the word you use when you need to make it intelligible to somebody whose principal frame of reference is measured polyphony.

The same is true of the expression "one note against another." The implied opposition here, surely, is to "more than one note against one." In other words, it implies an opposition to rhythmic differentiation. What has changed is not the practice as such, therefore, but the frame of reference within which it is understood. It is for similar reasons, for example, that we nowadays describe plainchant as "rhythmless" and "unmeasured," not because these are novel qualities that chant did not have long ago, but because they require explanation within a modern frame of musical reference that is conditioned almost wholly by rhythm and measure. It would be surprising to find similar terms used, say, in the tenth century.

All this is borne out by Petrus's musical example of *simplex discantus* (Example 1). The lowest voice-part here is labeled Tenor, exactly as it would have been labeled in regular discant. The tenor turns out to be based on a plainchant: it is *Kyrie fons bonitatis*. The other two voices both carry the label "contrapunctum," a clear indication that Petrus knew and used the word as a technical term. Once again, however, he seeks to make the musical realities intelligible within the framework of measured polyphony. The first of the two upper voices, he writes, is a counterpoint *quasi in loco tripli,* "as though in the place of a triplum," that is, the top part in a three-voice motet. And the second, he adds, is *loco moteti,* "in the place of the *motetus,*" that is, the middle part in a three-voice motet.

Example 1. Petrus dictus Palma ociosa, Compendium de discantu mensurabili *(c.1336): musical example of "contrapunctum." After Johannes Wolf, "Ein Beitrag zur Diskantlehre des 14. Jahrhunderts,"* Sammelbände der Internationalen Musikgesellschaft *15 (1913–14): 505-34*

From the example it is quite apparent that Petrus takes note-against-note singing to be unfamiliar to at least some of his readers. Those readers had to have the practice explained to them in terms of something they were evidently more familiar with—namely, the motet, and measured music in general. What Petrus seems to say here is this: just think of what you would do if you sang a motet. Now do the same, but forget everything about rhythm, and sing only whole notes, moving point against point. If you do that, it will sound like this (Example 2):

Example 2. Petrus dictus Palma ociosa, Compendium de discantu mensurabili *(c.1336): musical example of "contrapunctum," transcribed in modern notation*

Perhaps the contrast is not quite as dramatic, but still, to hear or play this example is to be reminded of Beethoven moving from Bonn to Vienna. Why would anyone in the early fourteenth century wish to sing whole-note counterpoints if what he was used to doing, or hearing, was motet-style polyphony? One answer could be, perhaps, that Petrus was a Cistercian monk; he had taken monastic vows, and among the things of this world that he had renounced, conceivably, was the kind of singing you did in motets.

But no, that is almost certainly not the answer. Petrus's treatise consists of three sections. Thus far we have only seen the first, which is wholly devoted to *simplex discantus*, note-against-note singing. The second is about *musica falsa*, the sorts of sharps we have just seen in his three-part counterpoint, and how and when you can introduce them. Then, in the third and final section, he turns to a new topic, which he calls "the flowers of measured music," that is, rhythmicized music. Let us read how he introduces this final topic (my italics):

> Sicut videmus arborem tempore aestatis adornatam et decoratam floribus et animam sanctam hominis virtutibus necnon etiam beatissimam virginem Mariam de incarnatione filii sui unigeniti sine corruptione, sic omnis discantus de floribus musicae mensurabilis adornatur et etiam decoratur. Dicunt enim flores musicae mensurabilis, quando plures voces seu notulae, quod idem est, diversimode figuratae secundum uniuscuiusque qualitatem ad unam vocem seu notulam simplicem tantum quantitatem illarum vocum continentem iusta proportione reducuntur.

> Just as we see the tree in summertime being adorned and decorated by blossoms, and the holy soul of a man by virtues, and indeed the most blessed Virgin by the incarnation without defilement of her only begotten Son, thus, in like manner, is all discant adorned and decorated by flowers of mensural music. Flowers of mensural music are so called *when several sounds or little notes* (which is the same thing), that are shaped differently each according to their quality, *are related in a just proportion to only one sound or plain note* that contains the quantity of those sounds.

What Petrus means is a kind of polyphony in which one voice still moves in whole notes, but the other one, the one on top, is broken up into small rhythmic values. He gives us no fewer than twelve examples of this practice, and it may be useful to consider just the first of these (Example 3). Interestingly, those "flowers of measured music" can be immediately recognized as a style of polyphony known and widely practiced for at least a century and a half: it is closely related to *organum purum*, the two-part organum in which one voice moves in long unmeasured notes, and the other in irregularly measured rhythms. How very odd: Petrus describes music of

Example 3. *Petrus dictus Palma ociosa,* Compendium de discantu mensurabili *(c.1336): "the first mode of measured discant adorned with flowerets," and note-against-note reduction of the same*

this kind as though it were something entirely new, even though this style, or some approximation of it, had existed long before. Something is not adding up here. If note-against-note counterpoint, *simplex discantus*, is something you might sing *in place of* a motet (which is what Petrus quite literally implied about his earlier example), and if we are to believe that *simplex discantus* is something that would have been suitable for Cistercian monks to practice, then why should he now go to the trouble of explaining how to turn it into elaborately rhythmicized discants? If it is alright to sing such music after all, then why not sing motets in the first place, instead of taking this elaborate and apparently redundant detour into note-against-note singing?

Petrus provides an answer to that question, yet one has to read between the lines to find it, for it is easy to miss. Example 3 may look like *organum purum*, but that's not actually what it is. If we take Petrus at his word, then it is an ornamented version of something else. To invoke his own analogies, when a tree is covered with cherry blossoms, it may be a greater pleasure for us to behold, and we may not be able to see the branches anymore, but it is still a tree. When the soul of a holy man is ornamented with virtues, he may resemble a heavenly being and seem like an angel, yet he is still a human. When the blessed Virgin gave birth to Jesus without defilement, she may have become the Mother of God, yet she was still a woman. And when discant is ornamented with flowers of measured music, it may sound like a motet, but it is still—well, what is it? What is it that still resides underneath all those ornaments? What would we be left with if we took them away?

The answer comes in a third important passage from Petrus's treatise. It turns out that *simplex discantus* had not, after all, been a useless diversion. After giving his twelve examples, of which we have just seen the first, Petrus emphasizes that all of them "are arranged from the same musical intervals from which *discantus simplex* is put together and arranged, and in the same manner" (my italics):

Quod siquidem XII modi sive maneries ex eisdem speciebus musicalibus, a quibus simplex discantus componitur et ordinatur, et isti similiter ordinati sunt, et nihilominus iste discantus claris, ut dictum est, floribus adornatus una cum speciebus musicalibus ante dictis quandoque descendit et ascendit vicissim per dissonantias, videlicet per semitonium, tonum, diatessaron, tritonum, semiditonum cum diapente, et ditonum cum diapente ...

The twelve modes or manners are *arranged from the same musical intervals from which plain discant is put together and arranged, and in the same manner*, yet nonetheless this discantus (being, as said before, adorned with bright flowers) falls and rises not just by the aforesaid musical intervals, but sometimes in turn by dissonances, that is, with the semitone, whole tone, fourth, augmented fourth, minor seventh, and major seventh ...

So if we took away the flowers, we should end up with *discantus simplex*, or counterpoint. And as a matter of fact we do (Example 4). The bottom part once again turns out to be a plainchant, the Sanctus from *Liber Usualis* Mass VIII, and the top voice accompanies it with fifths, octaves, sixths, and thirds. Apart from the octave parallels right there in the middle, which go back to measures 5 and 6, this is genuine first-species counterpoint. True, the top voice does leap about a lot, but then that is what it did also in Example 1, of which Petrus expressly said it was *discantus simplex*.

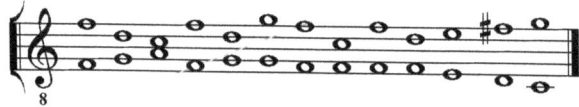

Example 4. Note-against-note reduction of Example 3

So here is what our Cistercian monk seems to be saying. When you are in church, and are about to sing the Kyrie or Sanctus, you may quite understandably wish to sing a motet, perhaps because you have done so throughout your life. But now suppose that for some reason you cannot sing a motet, perhaps because somebody has said you cannot. In that case it may still be fine to sing note-against-note polyphony, provided you follow the rules of counterpoint as they are laid out in this treatise. If, and only if, you follow those rules, then it may also be alright to add some flowers of measured music. But there are no shortcuts: do *not* skip the note-against-note stage.

If this is indeed what Petrus is implying, then one is bound to wonder: what could possibly be wrong or undesirable about singing a motet, and why would those flowers of measured music be any less wrong or undesirable? What is the difference anyway? That, unfortunately, is a question Petrus does not answer. Nor, in the next decades, do other theorists, even though they seem to be implying something very similar. Here, for example, is a passage from the slightly later *Ars contrapuncti* (c.1340–50) ascribed to Johannes de Muris. He gives the same definition of counterpoint as Petrus, and then he insists that this, *and only this*, is the true foundation of all polyphony (emphasis added):[11]

> Contrapunctus non est nisi punctum contra punctum ponere vel notam contra notam ponere vel facere, et est fundamentum discantus. Et quia sicut quis non potest edificare, nisi prius faciat fundamentum, sic aliquis non potest discantare, nisi prius faciat contrapunctum.
>
> *Counterpoint* is nothing but the setting of point against point, or the setting or making of note against note, and it *is the foundation of discant*. For just as someone cannot build unless he first lays a foundation, so *someone cannot sing discant unless he first makes counterpoint*.

Here is another author, the second Berkeley anonymous, who puts it yet another way (emphasis added):[12]

> Prius tamen notet unusquisque magistraliter discantare cupiens, regulas de contrapunctu supradictas debet super omnia observare. Nam licet communiter dicatur quod in verbulando, seu voces dividendo, bene possunt fieri due quinte, vel due duple, vel plures una post aliam, quia

---

11. After Edmond de Coussemaker, ed., *Scriptorum de musica medii aevi nova series a Gerbertina altera*, 4 vols. (Paris: Durand, 1864–1876), 3: 59.
12. After Oliver B. Ellsworth, ed. and trans., *The Berkeley Manuscript*, Greek and Latin Music Theory 2 (Lincoln: University of Nebraska Press, 1984), 130–31.

dicitur ibi fieri media. Ego tamen dico quod hoc faciens non magistraliter procedit.

First, however, *anyone who desires to sing discant in masterful manner must mark that he observe the aforesaid rules of counterpoint above all.* For although it is commonly said that in verbulating, or dividing up of notes, there can well be two fifths, or two octaves, or more, after one another, since it is said that there will be ones in between. I, on the other hand, say that someone doing this does not proceed masterfully.

Indirectly, this is a slap on the wrist of our first author, Petrus de Palma ociosa. When there are parallel octaves in your original counterpoint, some might defend them on the grounds that if you divide up the notes, or add flowers of measured music, there is going to be a long melisma between them anyway. So who would still be hearing those octaves? Would we have heard them in Example 3? Surely not. But no, says the Berkeley anonymous, you are not supposed to do that. Someone who moves in parallel octaves, like Petrus did in his two-voice example, mm. 5-6, is *not proceeding masterfully*.

All this adds up to a coherent picture, albeit a confusing one. Note-against-note singing seems to have received a reappreciation in the 1330s, and within two decades, theorists agreed that the new rules governing music on this level, the rules of counterpoint, were binding for all polyphony. Otherwise, you would not have laid a proper foundation, you would not be proceeding masterfully.

It is interesting to note, by the way, that there is a slightly authoritarian tone creeping in these discussions, an element even of intolerance. Once upon a time, a troubadour might reckon himself an accomplished musician if he was able to sing in every available style in church, even organum and counterpoint. Now, it is as if theorists are saying: forget about the other practices, we want you to sing only counterpoint. Their tone is not one of gentle persuasion, but rather of assertion. Yet in doing so they leave many questions unanswered—questions that we are evidently not supposed to ask. Why should counterpoint all of a sudden have to be the foundation of all polyphony? Says who? What is not masterful about parallel octaves when they are separated by

What is Counterpoint?

Example 5. Philippe de Vitry, isorhythmic motet *Firmissime fidem/Adesto/ Alleluya* (1310s), mm. 1–12, with reduction of sonorities per mensural unit

an elaborate melisma? Why is it alright to ornament *discantus simplex* with flowers of measured music, but not alright to sing an old-style motet? They never tell us. But from now on, clearly, this is how it's going to be.

Whatever the motives behind all this, composers do seem to have obeyed the theorists, or rather, perhaps, conspired with them. We can tell this from Example 5. It is a motet by Philippe de Vitry, dating probably from the early 1310s. The piece is highly ornate rhythmically, and so it might be tempting to compare it with the "flowers of measured music" that Petrus de Palma ociosa would be writing about two decades later. In the example, I have given not only the three voices of the motet, but also a reduction, in which the most ornate decorations have been removed. It will be obvious that what is left is not counterpoint, even if we set aside the fact that there are rhythms in all voices. The music moves firmly and unabashedly in parallel fifths and octaves—exactly the sort of thing that would no longer be considered masterful by the Berkeley anonymous. Even if Vitry had known counterpoint as an oral musical tradition at this early date, he does not seem to have accorded it any relevance to his written music.

Now jump ahead three decades, to 1342, the year in which the same Vitry composed his motet *Petre clemens*. Unfortunately I lack the space to print the whole piece, which is quite long, but Example 6 shows a reduction similar to the one I made earlier for Petrus de Palma ociosa and his flowers of measured music. That is to say, for every note in the cantus firmus, I took the first note that was sung over it in the other voices, no matter whether it was consonant or not, or whether it would be left with parallel fifths and octaves or not. Glancing over the end result, you will see that there are plenty of spots where this is clearly not proper counterpoint, where there are dissonances, parallels, or movement in unison. Yet the parallel fifth-octave sounds that made up the substance of the earlier motet have completely disappeared. We are a lot closer to the kind of three-part unmeasured counterpoint that we find in the treatise of Petrus de Palma ociosa.

What is Counterpoint?

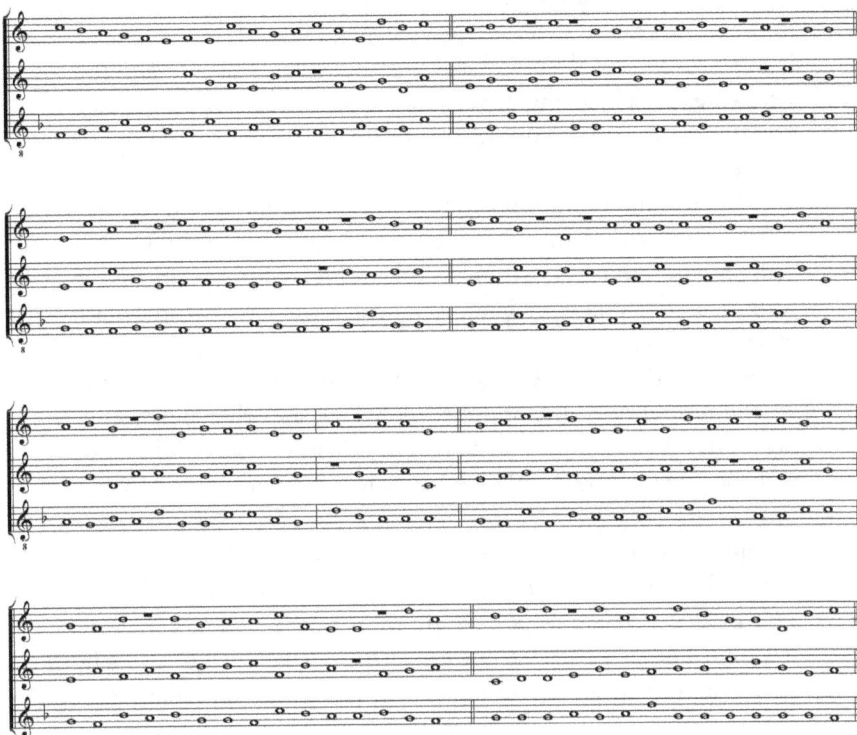

Example 6. Philippe de Vitry, Petre clemens / Lugentium siccentur / [Tenor] *(1342), note-against-tenor note reduction, excluding sections in hocket*

Partly because of this, I am no longer sure that by the 1340s, Vitry would never have heard of counterpoint, or would have doubted its relevance to written music. Certainly it would be very easy to reduce Vitry's motet in a way that would prove it to have an almost flawless contrapuntal foundation. But that would probably be a circular exercise, in that we would assume what is yet to be demonstrated. The reduction in Example 6 is not conclusive proof, but it is consistent enough with the theoretical record to suggest that something decisive really had taken place.

Let us now go back to the question with which we started the second section of this contribution: when counterpoint first emerges, I asked, what is new and distinctive about the art, and which of those new and distinctive things can still be recognized in the counterpoint that Beethoven learned several centuries later? Paradoxically, and despite the major break that I mentioned earlier—the one occurring around 1600—everything that was new and distinctive about counterpoint when it first emerged can still be recognized in Beethoven's lessons.

First of all, counterpoint moves in whole notes, exactly like the first-species counterpoint Beethoven learned from Haydn. The only difference is that medieval counterpoint was notated in unmeasured plainchant neumes, and Beethoven's counterpoint in whole notes.

Second, the basic note-against-note progressions were said to be the foundation, the starting point, for all other polyphony, no matter how complex in conception it might be. In the same way, Beethoven was not allowed to move on to the second species until he had mastered the first.

Finally, and not least important, there is the slightly authoritarian element in the curriculum. The theorists not only declare, as if by decree, that all polyphony must now be based on counterpoint, but they add that the only proper way to acquire it is by proceeding as they say you must, that is, by rigorous training in note-against-note singing, before you are even allowed to do anything else. It is they who set the curriculum, it is they who tell you what is valid and not valid, what is legitimate and not legitimate, and ultimately, what is music and is not music. Even Beethoven, for all the mastery in composition he so clearly possessed, had to go back to school and submit to this doctrinaire regime—in a curriculum so laughably simple that it seemed designed more to ritualize his unquestioning obedience than to foster meaningful compositional skills. The less sense it made to do the exercises, and the more arbitrary they seemed, the more effectively they brought home the unquestionable authority of the tradition.

Small wonder, then, that counterpoint, in the fourteenth century, rapidly became the world language in music, despite the many other dialects and idioms of medieval polyphony that we know once existed. We know of *quintizare* or fifthing, we know of melismatic organum, and discant, there are still reports, in the late thirteenth century, of singing in parallel octaves and fifths, and in Milan we even hear of a longstanding tradition of accompanying plainchants in fourths and seconds.[13] None of these traditions made bold claims to exclusive validity and authority, none of them aspired to universality, and all of them eventually disappeared. Counterpoint did not arrive on the scene simply as the latest flavor in polyphony, as something you were free to take or leave. It was there to become the gospel, the new dispensation, of all music other than plainchant. It was there to become an instrument of control, a tool with which to enforce uniformity and discipline in musical life, a tool with which to take offenders to task, and to keep newcomers in line.

So yes, there is continuity, even across the nearly five centuries that separate Beethoven from Vitry. And paradoxically, the elements that remain constant are precisely the ones that seem to point away from improvisation. Where, after all, is the living practice in all of this? Where is the idea of picking up an idiom like you would pick up a language? Why, even at this early date, did the cart of grammar come before the horse of living language? How do we reconcile all this with what I said before, that counterpoint had been a living practice throughout the fifteenth and sixteenth centuries, and became a dead language only later?

3.

There is a document that may help to resolve these questions. It is a text that that had been drafted and promulgated some eleven years before the treatise of Petrus de Palma ociosa, around 1325. We are still familiar with it, as what music historians have liked to describe as one of the most ineffective decrees ever issued in the history of the papacy. I am referring, of course, to *Docta sanctorum patrum*, the bull in which Pope John XXII at Avignon sought to curb musical practices in church that he and his college

---

13. See Rob C. Wegman, "Roads Taken and Not Taken in Medieval Music: The Case of False Counterpoint," in *Vom Preis des Fortschritts: Gewinn und Verlust in der Musikgeschichte*, ed. Andreas Dorschel and Andreas Haug, Studien zur Wertungsforschung 49 (Vienna: Universal Edition, 2008), 142–60, and the literature cited there.

of cardinals deemed unacceptable.[14] How and why could this text be relevant to the story of counterpoint?

First of all, it is important to remember that the bull was not an attack on church polyphony per se, and did not seek to ban it altogether. But anyone who wanted to observe its rulings—and the Pope threatened severe penalties for those who did not—would have to sing polyphony of a very different kind than he had been used to, or than could be practiced in society. The attack was really against rhythm. More specifically, it was targeted against any and all attempts to introduce rhythms in plainchant, or to notate chants in rhythmic values. Here is how the Pope himself puts it:

> Sed nonnulli novellae scholae discipuli, dum temporibus mensurandis invigilant, novis notis intendunt, fingere suas, quam antiquas cantare malunt, in semibreves et minimas ecclesiastica cantantur, notulis percutiuntur.

> But some disciples of a new school, occupying themselves with the measuring of time units, [now] signify with new notes, and prefer to make up their own rather than sing the old ones. The ecclesiastical [chants] are sung in semibreves and minims, and beaten with little notes.

That is the decree in a nutshell. What the Pope is saying is this: allow the plainchant to retain its dignity and gravity, by singing

---

14. For this and what follows, see Emil Friedberg, ed., *Corpus juris canonici*, 2 vols. (Leipzig: Bernhard Tauchnitz, 1879–81), 1: 18. Cf. Robert F. Hayburn, *Papal Legislation and Sacred Music, 95 A.D. to 1977 A.D.* (Collegeville, Minn.: Liturgical Press, 1979), 20–21. See also Franz Körndle, "Die Bulle 'Docta sanctorum patrum': Überlieferung, Textgestalt und Wirkung," *Musikforschung* 63 (2010): 147–65; id., "Liturgieverständnis an der Schwelle zur Neuzeit: Die Bulle 'Docta sanctorum patrum' Papst Johannes' XXI. und ihre Anwendung," in Klaus Pietschmann, ed., *Papsttum und Kirchenmusik vom Mittelalter bis zu Benedikt XVI.: Positionen, Entwicklungen, Kontexte* (Kassel and New York: Bärenreiter, 2012), 67–80; id., "Michael Praetorius und die Tradition der katholischen Kirchenmusik," in Susanne Rode-Breymann and Arne Spohr, ed., *Michael Praetorius – Vermittler europäischer Musiktraditionen um 1600*, Ligaturen: Musikwissenschaftliches Jahrbuch der Hochschule für Musik, Theater und Medien Hannover (Hildesheim, Zurich, and New York: Olms, 2011), 67–83.

it in the old neumes, the notes that are unmeasured. At first sight this does not sound like a principled attack against polyphony per se. If you promise to keep the plainchant unmeasured, there is still a lot you can do in the second voice-part. For example, Pope John might well have approved of the old *organum purum*, the style of polyphony in which the plainchant notes were not only kept unmeasured, but notated in their original neumes. Still, this did not give singers a license to do as they pleased. For here is how the Pope went on:

> Nam melodias hoquetis intersecant, discantibus lubricant, triplis et motetis vulgaribus nonnumquam inculcant adeo, ut interdum antiphonarii et gradualis fundamenta despiciant, ignorent, super quo aedificant, tonos nesciant, quos non discernunt, immo confundunt, quum ex earum multitudine notarum adscensiones pudicae, descensionesque temperatae, plani cantus, quibus toni ipsi secernuntur ad invicem, obfuscentur.
>
> For they cut the melodies with hockets, make them slippery with discants, and sometimes add vernacular *tripla* and *moteti*, to such a degree that at times they spurn or disregard the very foundations of the Antiphonal and Gradual on which they build, [that they] are unaware of the church modes, which they do not distinguish but rather confuse, because the modest ascents and measured descents of the plainchant, by which those modes are distinguished from one another, are obscured by the multitude of those notes.

So polyphony can be problematic, even when the plainchant is kept unmeasured. There is a problem, for example, when the original plainchant ends up being smothered with such rhythmic busywork in the other voices that you cannot tell anymore what mode it is in. Although the Pope does not expressly forbid rhythms in the other voices, it is clear that the degree of rhythmic elaboration will have to be reduced significantly. And he is quite categorical about the adding of voices such as *motetus* and *triplum*, which carry texts in vernacular languages. This is unacceptable—no ifs and buts. Since these are the typical voice-parts in motets, it follows that the motet has no place in church. It is banned, as per the decree of the Holy Father.

Against the background of this Papal decree, some of the things in the treatise of Petrus de Palma ociosa begin to make apparent sense. For example, when Petrus implies, in the passage cited earlier, that you can sing counterpoints, literally, "in the place of a *triplum*," or "in the place of a *motetus*," he seems to be addressing musicians who are used to singing *tripla* and *moteti*, and who for some reason are looking for an alternative. The only problem, of course, is that Petrus offers an alternative in note-against-note counterpoint, without rhythm in any voice. And so far, we have not heard the Pope say that this is the only acceptable way of singing polyphony in church.

It is hard to know if that is in fact what John XXII meant to enforce with his decree. Yet the Pope comes very close to it in the final paragraph of his bull, where he specifies the sort of polyphony that may still be sung without penalty. Now his words give the impression that he had almost been ready to banish every kind of polyphony, but decided, seemingly as an afterthought, to retreat from this position of excessive severity. For we see him making a number of concessions which, if taken literally, would curtail church polyphony to something very basic and primitive indeed. Here is how he puts it:

> Per hoc autem non intendimus prohibere, quin interdum diebus festis praecipue, sive solemnibus in missis et praefatis divinis officiis aliquae consonantiae, quae melodiam sapiunt, puta octavae, quintae, quartae et huiusmodi supra cantum ecclesiasticum simplicem proferantur, sic tamen, ut ipsius cantus integritas illibata permaneat, et nihil ex hoc de bene morata musica immutetur, maxime quum huiusmodi consonantiae auditum demulceant, devotionem provocent, et psallentium Deo animos torpere non sinant.

> With all this, however, we do not intend to prohibit that once in a while, especially on feastdays and holidays, during Mass or in the aforesaid Holy Offices, some consonances that have the savor of melodious sound, such as octave, fifth, fourth, and others of this kind, be sung over the simple ecclesiastical chant—provided, however, that the integrity of the chant shall remain unimpaired, and that nothing of this well-ordered music be changed in any way. This above all because consonances of this kind soothe the hearing, stir devotion, and do not allow the minds of those who are singing to God to become torpid.

Does this amount to a prohibition of all rhythm in polyphony? It is hard to be sure. What is definitely being prohibited, without any ambiguity or qualification, is dissonance. And in a way that comes down to the same thing. At this time, the only known styles of polyphony that made use exclusively of consonance, without any admixture of dissonance, were parallel organum in fourths, fifths and octaves, and note-against-note counterpoint.

So there is a mixed message. On the one hand, the Pope is calling for radical change in those churches where motets, hockets, and other new-fangled rhythmic trash could be heard on a regular basis. All of that will have to go. On the other hand, he positively encourages singing in consonances, provided that the plainchant remains unmeasured, and is not drowned in a lavish profusion of small notes, or stained with dissonances. There seems to be a little wiggle room here, but not a great deal. The precise interpretation of the rulings would have been up to bishops, who were charged with enforcing the Pope's decree in their respective dioceses, and with handing out punishments where appropriate. In those dioceses where note-against-note singing was practiced in preference to measured polyphony, it is not hard to imagine a bishop translating the decree in practical terms that clerics could immediately understand, by saying that this was the only thing that would still be safe to practice. That would not have been an unreasonable interpretation of the bull. And those clerics who were unfamiliar with note-against-note singing either had to find others who could teach it to them, or get somebody to write up the rules.

This scenario would explain a number of things. It would explain, first of all, why a practice that had existed, up to then, only as an oral tradition, namely, singing "contrapontamens," became one whose rules needed to be codified in writing. It would also explain one of the curious paradoxes about counterpoint. On the one hand, the rules are so childishly simple that you would imagine the curriculum was intended really for beginning choirboys. On the other hand, those same rules were written up in Latin treatises, a medium aimed at clerics rather than six-year-old boys. The typical counterpoint treatise, at least in the fourteenth century, seems to answer to the needs of those who had to undergo reschooling, or of those who had to teach them.

What I am suggesting, in other words, is that basic note-against-note counterpoint came to be privileged, in the Catholic Church, as the safe alternative to the polyphonic practices that the Pope had firmly prohibited. There is in fact some evidence that seems to bear out this hypothesis. A few decades ago, Giulio Cattin drew attention to a medieval tradition of basic note-against-note polyphony that he referred to as *cantus planus binatim*—which can be translated roughly as "plainchant doubled."[15] The idea is that the plainchant is accompanied by a second voice which behaves exactly like plainchant, in unmeasured notes, written in neumes—like the *discantus simplex* discussed by Petrus de Palma ociosa. These kinds of primitive two-part singing are found almost exclusively in liturgical manuscripts, books that are wholly devoted to plainchant proper. Occasionally in these books, you will find a chant in which every neume is accompanied by another neume above it in the same staff, usually at a distance of a fourth, fifth, or octave. And this practice was widespread: it is found everywhere in Europe, in France, the Netherlands, Germany, Poland, Italy, and elsewhere. Once again, it turns out, note-against-note singing is not a pointless diversion: it was actually practiced in the everyday liturgy, especially (judging from the provenance of the sources) in monasteries.

Cantus planus binatim is usually said to have emerged some time around the late thirteenth and early fourteenth centuries. It would be rash on my part to claim that it emerged only towards the end of this timespan, in direct response to the papal bull of 1325. On the other hand, the bull has often been described as ineffective, but if we are to determine its real impact, surely the sources for this kind of polyphony could be among the most pertinent evidence we have.

I have emphasized that Pope John XXII did not specifically say that counterpoint would henceforth be the only acceptable kind of polyphony—only that this would have been a reasonable interpretation of the document on the part of contemporary bishops. And

---

15. Gallo, F Alberto: "'Cantus Planus Binatim': Polifonia Primitiva in Fonti Tardive: Firenze, BN, II XI 18; Washington, LC, ML 171 J 6; Firenze, BN, Pai. 472," *Quadrivium* 7 (1966): 79–89.

it would not surprise me if that interpretation had been enforced in many dioceses, at least in France. On the other hand, this hard-line stance must soon have given way to compromise. It is easy to imagine the protests among clerics after a few years of singing the liturgy in this way. Is it really not alright to sing rhythms in voices other than the plainchant? Did the Pope actually say that in so many words? Well, it's not so clear—we have just seen that the bull is lacking in precision on precisely this point. So it is easy to imagine a bishop saying, maybe already within the first decade: alright, you can add flowers of measured music, *provided* you make absolutely sure the starting point is still note-against-note singing in consonances. I do not want to hear any motets.

This might help to explain the odd circumspection with which Petrus de Palma ociosa introduced the topic of those flowers. Why would he liken his rhythmicized organum-style elaborations to, respectively, a tree in bloom, a holy man adorned with virtues, and indeed even with the Virgin Mary—when all we hear is something very similar to the top voice in a motet? The answer lies precisely in that deceptive similarity. Because the flowers so much resemble the kind of music that Pope John XXII had outlawed, they now need an elaborate justification of their own. And the justification, for Petrus, is that you're still, in a way, singing *simplex discantus*, except that it has been made even prettier than it already was. More importantly, we have seen him emphasizing, in the third quote, that the examples "are arranged from the same musical intervals from which *discantus simplex* is arranged, and in the same manner."

Why is that so important? Well, remember what Pope John XXII had said: "we do not intend to prohibit that once in a while ... a few consonances ... such as octave, fifth, fourth, and others of this kind, are sung over the ecclesiastical plainchant." Petrus is at pains, it seems, to observe the letter of the decree. Of course, his reasoning here is clumsy and awkward, and frankly unconvincing, which is exactly why the poetic similes he invokes are so completely over the top. Do we really need to compare his flowers of measured music to the Virgin Mary in order to be persuaded that they have merit? Well, if you lived in the 1330s, then quite possibly you did. After all, *Docta sanctorum patrum* did promise an eight-day suspension for those clerics who failed to heed its rulings.

Let us take stock before moving on. In Section Two of this contribution, I have identified a number of traits that were new and distinctive about counterpoint when it first emerged in the 1330s, and that can still be recognized in Beethoven's time. First of all, counterpoint has no rhythm, it moves only in whole notes. Second, the note-against-note singing that results from this is said to be the foundation of all polyphony, and must be the first thing that any student of counterpoint learns before moving on to other things. Finally, there is the slightly authoritarian element, the claim to exclusive validity, and the rejection of other kinds of polyphony.

In Section Three I have argued that counterpoint became the privileged musical language in church after the bull *Docta sanctorum patrum* of 1325, and that this event could ultimately explain those three traits, as well as a number of other things—the fact that counterpoint became the world language in music, the fact that its rules were codified in Latin treatises, and the emergence of *cantus planus binatim*.

Still, there is an important question that remains unanswered. For I have also noted that these very traits seem to be pointing away from improvisation, from the idea of picking up counterpoint like you pick up a language. Theorists seem to have agreed, throughout history, from the 1330s to the present day, that "picking up the language" is *not* the way to learn counterpoint at all. You cannot just sing along: you have to take lessons, you have to learn the grammar before you are allowed to speak. How do we reconcile this with what I argued in Section One—that counterpoint had been a living language before 1600? It is this question to which I will turn in the next section.

4.

The decree *Docta sanctorum patrum*, issued by Pope John XXII in 1325, was obviously ineffective, certainly in the long run. As early as the middle of the fourteenth century, we find Mass movements composed entirely in the manner of isorhythmic motets—the very thing that Pope John seems to have condemned in the most specific terms. Among the best-known examples, of course, are the isorhythmic movements in the *Messe de Nostre Dame* of Guillaume de Machaut, composed around 1370.

So at best, at least in the interpretation I have offered here, the papal decree had ensured that all church polyphony—both written and improvised, simple and complex—would henceforth take its basis, its foundation, in the simple note-against-note polyphony that the Pope had positively endorsed. Or at least in one particular idiom of such polyphony, counterpoint. Machaut's Mass is once again a good example. Margaret Bent has convincingly demonstrated that the various movements of this cycle observe the rules of counterpoint almost to the letter.[16] So if my reading of *Docta sanctorum patrum* is correct—and I should emphasize that it is, of course, only a hypothesis—then the papal bull does seem to have been effective in at least this regard.

On the other hand, when Medieval and Renaissance music theorists had occasion to look back upon that old decree, and reflected upon its stern warnings against the rhythmic excesses of contemporary church music, it was obvious to them that Pope's rulings had had no effect on musical practice at all. And it was equally obvious that his decree would be far too drastic and too crippling a measure to implement belatedly, at least within the Catholic Church.

Yet there are exceptions. There are theorists who give us fresh or arresting perspectives on the Papal bull. One of these is a German music theorist by the name of Seth Calvisius. In the year 1600 he published at Leipzig a compendium of basic music theory entitled *Exercitationes musicae duae*. The final section of this treatise offered a review of the history of music theory, based on any and all sources he was able to lay his hands on. One of those sources happens to be *Docta sanctorum patrum*. Calvisius was fascinated by the text, which he treated, interestingly, as a historical rather than ecclesio-political document. He knew next to nothing about the musical world of the early fourteenth century, and

---

16. Margaret Bent, "The 'Harmony' of the Machaut Mass," in Elizabeth Eva Leach, ed., *Machaut's Music New Interpretations*, Studies in Medieval and Renaissance Music (Woodbridge, UK: Boydell & Brewer, 2003), 75–94.

so he was all the more intrigued to learn from the pope's bull that people had already been using such notes as semibreves and minims at this early date. At the same time he concluded that those notes must have been recent inventions, since Pope John ascribed their creation to "the disciples of a new school." Calvisius did not think that church music around 1325 could have been very interesting. After all, what sort of music can you write when all you have is semibreves and minims, without the semiminims, fusae, semifusae, and even smaller values that were available in his time? Nor was Calvisius much encouraged by the Pope's complaints about the ridiculous antics of singers, their blatant disregard of the church modes, and their evident unconcern with the rhetorical powers of music. Good thing that Pope John had put a stop to all that.

There was also something else Calvisius was interested to learn from the bull. It has to do with the passage in which Pope John XXII seemed to be stepping back from a position of excessive severity, and allowed, even encouraged, the singing of consonances along with the plainchant notes, provided that those notes be kept integral and unrhythmicized. Here is that passage once again:

> With all this, however, we do not intend to prohibit that once in a while, especially on feastdays and holidays, during Mass or in the aforesaid Holy Offices, some consonances that have the savor of melodious sound, such as octave, fifth, fourth, and others of this kind, be sung over the simple ecclesiastical chant—provided, however, that the integrity of the chant shall remain unimpaired, and that nothing of this well-ordered music be changed in any way. This above all because consonances of this kind soothe the hearing, stir devotion, and do not allow the minds of those who are singing to God to become torpid.

Reading this very passage nearly three hundred years later, Calvisius had not the slightest doubt as to what it meant. "Here," he said,[17]

---

17. Seth Calvisius, *Exercitationes musicae duae. Qvarvm prior est, de modis mvsicis, qvos vulgò Tonos vocant, rectè cognoscendis, et dijudicandis. Posterior, de initio et progressv Mvsices, alijsque rebus eo spectantibus* (Leipzig: Iacobus Apelius, 1600), 132–33.

...Pontifex, choralem cantum fundamentum facit consonantiarum addendarum, unde procul dubio non alia Harmonia exorietur, quam contrapunctus extemporaneus, ut vocant, sive Harmonia, quae posset dici αυτοσχεδιασική, quando videlicet, qui graviorem sonum proferre possunt, choralem cantum simpliciter canunt. Reliqui vero, qui voce acutiores sunt, consonantias, octavas, quintas et quartas, pro libitu, non praemeditati addunt, quod apud concentores aulicos quosdam in capellis, ut vocant, et in quibusdam coenobijs apud Pontificios hodie in usu est. Quanquam hi de quibus Pontifex loquitur, fortassis ex praescripto, ut minus exercitati consonantias miscuerunt.

...the Pope established plainchant as the foundation of the consonances that are to be added. From which, without any doubt, no other kind of music could be born than extemporized counterpoint, or that harmony which is called "autoschediastic" [improvised]. That is to say, when those who have deeper voices sing the plainchant *simpliciter* [that is to say, in whole notes, unbroken, *simplex*], yet the others, who have higher voices, add consonances, octaves, fifths, and fourths, at will, without forethought—just as is the custom today among certain court singers in chapels and in certain monasteries, and among Papal singers. Still, the singers of whom Pope [John] speaks, being less well trained, mingled their consonances perhaps from notation.

What a curious interpretation. Calvisius comes close to suggesting that Pope John XXII, by issuing his bull *Docta sanctorum patrum*, had single-handedly instituted the art of improvised counterpoint—a tradition, he notes, that wais still widely in use in the late sixteenth century, in court chapels, monasteries, even at the papal court. Calvisius concedes that the tradition may not have been very sophisticated when it began, and that the earliest singers may well have needed notation to help them along. But the point about the tradition, for him, is that it is one of improvisation: our music theorist sees precisely that point, improvisation, as the necessary consequence of the papal decree. If he is right, then *Docta sanctorum patrum* may have been far more effective than we could have imagined even earlier on.

But is he right? Why should Seth Calvisius, writing in 1600, be an especially informative guide to a papal bull that had been issued nearly three centuries before him? He may have been closer to it in time than we are, but greater chronological proximity does not necessarily confer special interpretive authority on his reading. On the other hand, sometimes we do need an early commentator—and especially one who was still familiar with counterpoint as a living tradition—to suggest a possibility that might not otherwise have occurred to us.[18] Consider just this. I concluded Section Three by noting an apparent contradiction: that counterpoint seems to have been a bookish art from the very beginning, that it was marked, already in the 1330s, by a note-against-note pedagogy so basic and restrictive that it seemed designed to stifle the freedom to improvise rather than to foster it. And this pedagogy was set up as the narrow gate through which every singer of polyphony had to pass—even if he wanted to add flowers of measured music, as Petrus de Palma ociosa said, or if he wanted to sing complex discant, as in the Muris and Berkeley texts. In order to pass through that gate, it seems, you must unlearn everything you ever did, and like Beethoven, start with the basics. And yet, counterpoint was a living practice throughout the fifteenth and sixteenth centuries. How do we reconcile all this?

Taking our cue from Calvisius, however, there may also be another way of looking at it. Let us take a few steps back. It is true that note-against-note counterpoint, or *discantus simplex*, does not necessarily have to be improvised: it can also exist as a written tradition. In Section Three I mentioned the example of *cantus planus binatim*, the simple polyphony written up in liturgical manuscripts, which may have been notated for those

---

18. On the other hand, it is worth noting that he is not the only contemporary witness to offer this interpretation of the decree. See, for example, Michael J. Noone, *Music and Musicians in the Escorial Liturgy under the Habsburgs, 1563-1700* (Rochester, N.Y.: University of Rochester Press, 1998), 94–100, concerning the discussion of fabordón in Martín de la Vera, *Instrucion de eclesiasticos* (Madrid: Emprenta Real, 1630), 195–96. See also Sébastien de Brossard, *Dictionaire de Musique, Contenant une Explication Des Termes Grecs, Latins, Italiens et François les plus usitez dans la Musique* (3rd ed.; Amsterdam: Estienne Roger, 1708), 318: "Sur le Livre; Chanter sur le Livre. ... Je croy que l'origine en vient pour les Eglises, d'une Decretale du Pape Jean XXII. qui commence Docta Sanctorum Patrum decrevit authoritas et cetera."

monks who could not handle the rules of counterpoint effortlessly. On the other hand, note-against-note is not really the kind of polyphony of which a trained singer would be inclined to write down many specimens, or of which you might want to collect a canon of classics.

So it should not surprise us that counterpoint seems to have originated as a wholly oral tradition. It never needed to be anything other than point-against-point: if you wanted to do something more adventurous, there were other idioms of polyphony around. But now imagine that all those other idioms are suddenly outlawed, at least in the church, and that counterpoint is declared to be the only proper way of singing church polyphony. Now if you want to do something more adventurous, there no longer is any other style to turn to. If you still want to do it, then of necessity you will have to claim that what you are doing is somehow still counterpoint—except that something decorative has been added to it, like cherry blossoms decorating a tree. That is why the "flowers of measured music" of which Petrus de Palma ociosa spoke in 1336 are emphatically not old-style motets or organa, however similar they may sound as far as their rhythms are concerned. And they differ also in another respect. Unlike motets, which are a *written* genre by definition, you would never need to write down those flowers, for they really were decorative, cosmetic, and inessential outside of performance. The only exception is when you were writing a treatise, and you needed to give an example of how to do it. That is precisely what Petrus de Palma ociosa says about his own twelve examples, the first of which was printed above. Petrus immediately admits that there are too many possibilities to write them all down—which is another good reason why it would be pointless to compose anything in this style. As as he puts it:[19]

> Quamvis autem nonnulli dicant et affirment flores scientiae musicalis fore innumerabiles secundum diversos modos discantus, et de innumerabilibus non valet haberi certitudo, nolentes ob hanc causam de floribus huiusmodi aliquam artem componere. Tamen ne iuvenes

---

19. Op. cit., 517.

et alii cupientes in dicta scientia proficere aliquam artem de eadem non habentes ob hoc fiant tepidi et remissi istam scilicet addiscendo, idcirco ego circa capacitatem ingenioli mei XII modos seu maneries de discantu mensurabili floribus adornato compilavi.

Now although some will say and affirm that the flowers of the discipline of music are innumerable according to the different modes of discant, and certainty cannot be had from things that are innumerable, and are for that reason unwilling to put together a treatise about flowers of this kind, still, in order that youths and others who desire to become proficient in the said discipline, yet who do not have access to some treatise about it, might not become sluggish and lazy when learning it, I have put together, within the limits of my little wit, twelve modes or manners of measurable discant adorned with flowers.

Now who would those young people, and others eager for the said knowledge, be? Certainly they must be singers who can already produce note-against-note counterpoint, for that is the necessary foundation for the art of adding flowers. So they must be clerics, and their eagerness to play around with the basic note-against-note progressions must stem precisely from the musical limitations of those progressions. They wanted something more—and in truth one cannot blame them. So there is one thing we can fairly sure of: the treatise of Petrus de Palma ociosa, which is the earliest counterpoint text we have, is not addressed to composers, it is addressed to singers. It teaches an art of contrapuntal improvisation.

The only problem for these clerics, and for theorists as well, was a semantic one. Counterpoint means literally: point against point. That is its distinctive feature, and that is the reason why it may have been privileged in the wake of *Docta sanctorum patrum*. The minute you start adding flowers of measured music, you no longer have counterpoint, at least not in the literal sense. Petrus de Palma ociosa is aware of that, but he prefers not to be too literal-minded about this. At bottom, he says, his twelve examples still are counterpoint, or *discantus simplex*, and that is how you should sing them. You could call it a form of creative denial, and it is not hard to imagine where this will lead. If you can safely add flowers of measured music to the basic counterpoints you're singing every day, then musically gifted clerics will soon seek to excel in the very art of doing so, and push the practice to unprecedented heights of musical sophistication—though never in writing, always in improvisation. In some churches, undoubtedly, the original note-against-note style would soon have been left behind, even if it remained a key part of the pedagogy, as the necessary foundation and legitimation of all polyphony. Now as this development goes on, it is only natural for the word counterpoint to be used in a looser sense, and for it to comprise, eventually, every form of polyphony that can claim to be rooted in that foundation. This is the sense in which we use the word still today, and why we need a pleonasm like note-against-note counterpoint. And most of that counterpoint will have developed, at least initially, in the realm of improvisation rather than composition.

So this is the insight we owe to Seth Calvisius and his reading, in 1600, of *Docta sanctorum patrum*. Pope John XXII, by effectively banning all church polyphony that was written in new-fangled note-values, only caused those same rhythmic styles of singing to re-enter through the back door—the door of improvised note-against-note singing, which as a result grew into a massive gateway. One could probably say that in doing so, he gave a decisive impulse to the art of contrapuntal improvisation in church, and indirectly caused it to become the widely-practiced living musical language that it would remain for the next several centuries. It was an art that would always remain faithful to its origin and its foundation: the pedagogy of note-against-note singing. But on that foundation, it erected an elaborate structure that remained intricately connected with the world of improvised singing, even when composed music would eventually branch off and develop into a separate art. And if that is indeed how we can see it, then we have answered the question with which I ended my Section Three. Counterpoint, from the very beginning, was *both* bookish and improvised, both theory and practice.

5.

Unfortunately, what we have inherited from the Middle Ages and Renaissance is only the written tradition, and the pedagogy of the dead language that counterpoint has become. The oral tradition has died out, even though *chant sur le livre* is reported to have been practiced in French churches as late as the nineteenth century. As a consequence, music historians find themselves in a paradoxical situation. If they wish to come to an understanding of that lost oral tradition, they must of necessity turn to written traces. And that seems like a hopeless undertaking. Imagine trying to recover and relive the world of Bebop if all we had was the few transcriptions that some contemporaries might have committed to paper. Transcriptions can never substitute for the live experience. They give us traces of what was heard, yet they distort those traces at the same time.

Let me give an example to illustrate some of the problems we're dealing with. Figure 1 shows the preface and first page of a set of partbooks printed in Venice in 1574. It is a collection of liturgical music, and it is extremely rare—as far as I know the only surviving copy in the world is kept in the Royal Library in Brussels. The print is devoted to polyphonic Introits for several major feasts in the liturgical calendar, in settings ranging from four to six parts. The author—if that is the right word—is Hippolito Chamaterò di Negri, choirmaster at the Duomo of Udine, and a direct contemporary of Palestrina. In the preface, Chamaterò explains that the settings that follow are essentially records, transcriptions, of an improvised practice that could be heard in the Duomo under his direction, and which reportedly provoked considerable admiration amongst those who heard them.[20]

---

20. Hippolito Chamaterò di Negri, *Li introiti fondati sopra il canto fermo del basso* (Venice: l'herede di Girolamo Scotto, 1574), Bassus Partbook, 2–3.

Figure 1. Ippolito Chamaterò di Negri, Hippolito Chamaterò di Negri, Li introiti fondati sopra il canto fermo del basso *(Venice: l'herede di Girolamo Scotto, 1574), BassusPartbook, 2–3*

> ... quando era al seruitio del suo honorato Domo, non poco si delettauano della Musica dell' introiti, & che gioiuano à veder li miei scholari in choro nel far contraponti all' improuiso l'vn l'altro auanciarsi.
>
> ... when I was formerly in the service of the honored Duomo, people took no small delight in the music of the Introits, and rejoiced in seeing my choirboys rival with one another in the making of counterpoints *all'improviso*.

If we are to take Chamaterò at his word, then, his collection should give us a reliable idea of improvised polyphony as it could typically be heard in Italy in the late sixteenth century. After all, his print is dedicated to the canons of the Duomo of Udine, so if those canons were to believe him, the settings should bear more than a passing resemblance to what those same canons had heard in live performances in their own church. So let us consider an example from the collection, the Introit for Easter Sunday, *Resurrexi* (Appendix 1).

If we could take a time machine, and visit the Duomo of Udine on Easter Sunday 1574, is this a fair approximation of what we would have heard? It sounds almost too good to be true. The counterpoint is flawless, there are no awkward dissonances, there are no parallel fifths and octaves that stand out conspicuously, and, as if all that were not enough, the polyphony is marvelously rich in imitative gestures, picked up from voice to voice. It strains credibility that even the most thoroughly trained singers and choirboys in the sixteenth century would have been able to produce something of such contrapuntal polish and perfection, and that not from these partbooks, but fresh, spontaneous, on the spot. Surely, in everyday life there would have been clashes, parallels, wrongly timed imitations. True, Chamaterò could not be expected to provide an accurate reflection of such errors in a print that was meant be useful to others. Yet notwithstanding his disclaimer, we may have to insist that his print is likely, at best, to contain heavily edited versions of the real thing.

If this is indeed our response, then certainly we are not alone. There are writers from this very period, the late sixteenth century, who report similar responses. And just as in our own case, interestingly, these are responses from people for whom the tradition is no longer alive, who have no direct acquaintance with it. They try to imagine what improvised counterpoint would probably sound like, and they cannot bring themselves to believe that the music would not have been painful to listen to. The first author is Adrian Petit Coclico, the notorious self-declared student of Josquin des Prez, writing in 1552. For a man living in Germany, he considers himself a musician of the old school, for he still knows how to extemporize counterpoint, in fact he considers it an absolutely essential skill for any self-respecting musician. But alas, things are no longer what they used to be: the art has declined, and by now, in the middle of the sixteenth century, no-one in Germany believes that it is even worth trying to learn it, since it could not possibly result in anything the ears could bear. Here is how he puts it:[21]

> Modus canendi contrapunctum in Germania rarus est, haud dubie non aliam ob causam, quàm cum pulcherrima haec ars, diuturno usu, ac labore maximo perdiscatur, nec praemia eam callentibus con-stituta sint: perpauci ad hanc discendam animum applicent, solide se in Musica doctos existimantes, si uariorum signorum, prolationum, definitionum et caetera noticiam habuerint. Aut si cantilenam in anni spatio componant, quam uix canere possint. Ac si quis contrapuncti mentionem faciat, ac in perfecto Musico requirat, hunc odio plusquam canino lacerant, impudenter affirmantes, in contrapuncto multas prauas et corruptas species occurrere, quae aures offendant, et in compositionibus locum non habent.

> The manner of singing counterpoint is rare in Germany, undoubtedly because this most beautiful art can only be acquired through daily practice, and with the greatest effort, and because there are no rewards for those skilled in it. The very few who devote themselves to its study reckon that they are wholly learned in music if they know something about the various signs, prolations, definitions, etc., or if they take a year to compose a song that they could scarcely even sing. And if someone were to mention counterpoint, or expects it in the accomplished musician, they scorn him with more contempt than they would a dog, asserting shamelessly that there are many faulty and improper intervals occurring in counterpoint which offend the ears, and which have no place in composition.

---

21. Adrianus Petit Coclico, *Compendium musices* (Nuremberg: Berg and Neuber, 1552), f.Iiiijr.

And here, a few decades later, is Thomas Morley, in his famous *Plaine and Easie Introduction to Practicall Musicke*, of 1597. Morley is aware that it was once the custom in England to improvise counterpoint, and that it is still the custom elsewhere. But he is unable to believe that such music will not sound chaotic for most of the time, and he writes,[22]

> As for singing vppon a plainsong, it hath byn in times past in England (as euery man knoweth) and is at this day in other places, the greatest part of the vsuall musicke which in any churches is sung. Which indeed causeth me to maruel how men acquainted with musicke, can delight to heare such confusion as of force must bee amongste so many singing extempore. But some haue stood in an opinion which to me seemeth not very probable, that is, that men accustomed to descanting will sing together vpon a plainsong, without singing eyther false chords or forbidden descant one to another, which til I see I will euer think vnpossible.

Now, it may be reassuring to learn that we may not be alone in thinking this, and that there were people who already thought like this even in the sixteenth century, but actually it is also somewhat disconcerting. This response, the response of incredulity, clearly is typical of those who are not, or no longer, familiar with the tradition of contrapuntal improvisation, and so it probably says more about them—and us—than about the tradition as such. Other sixteenth-century writers who *are* familiar with the tradition, such as for example Zarlino, will sometimes complain about bad singers, or bad practices in contrapuntal improvisation—like singing the same motive incessantly, regardless of what other voices are doing. But they do not doubt for a second that counterpoint can and should sound magnificent when it is improvised properly. If they could have seen the music printed in Chamaterò's collection of Introits, maybe they would not have been incredulous at all. Perhaps it really is our fault, our limitation, and we should be willing to entertain the possibility, however counter-intuitive it might seem.

---

22. Thomas Morley, *A Plaine and Easie Introduction to Practicall Musicke* (London: Peter Short, 1597), fol. (:.) 1r.

Let us for a moment imagine that the music printed in the Appendix really is a close approximation of improvised polyphony. Is there anything that might confirm that this is indeed plausible, anything that makes the music recognizable as typically improvised, rather than composed? I believe there are several such features, and the most important of these is in the bass. It sings the plainchant for the Introit *Resurrexi*, and it does so consistently in half notes, which is my transcription for what were originally values corresponding to the semibreve. Except for two passages, beginning in measures 59 and 94, respectively, it does not move in any other rhythmic values. So this is a genuine cantus firmus, totally unornamented, and consistently rhythmicized in semibreves. Also, and no less significant, it has no rests. This in fact is critical in a piece that purports to reflect the practice of improvisation. The minute there is no cantus firmus, there is no anchor point against which to improvise consonances, and for someone singing in this style, that must be like the floor dropping out from under your feet.

Now all these features in the cantus firmus, in the voice labelled bassus, result from an interesting notational peculiarity. If we take another look at Figure 1, which shows the first opening of the bassus part book, we can see that the notes on the right-hand page are actually the ones that were sung in the setting in Appendix 1. They are not semibreves, however, but plainchant neumes. So for the bassus, the music looks exactly as it would have looked if he had been singing from the original plainchant manuscript, and if his colleagues had been inventing counterpoint on the spot. Their partbooks, on the other hand, are written in regular mensural notation, with semibreves, minims, and semiminims. So the idea is really that the plainchant is sung just the way it is, in unmeasured neumes, but that it is enveloped in rhythmicized counterpoints which, purely for their own reference, sing against each plainchant note as though it were a semibreve.

Why would Chamaterò have gone to the trouble of printing this notational peculiarity, when he might just as well have printed the bass voice in semibreves? In light of the historical background sketched here, it is tempting to suppose that he had perhaps obtained a copy of *Docta sanctorum patrum*, the papal bull from

1325, and chose to take its recommendations absolutely literally. That is to say, whatever singers were allowed to do in the other voices, one could not mess with the plainchant. It has to be kept in its original neumes. Its dignity and gravity must be maintained.

If Chamaterò's print were the only evidence we had, that would certainly have been quite a leap for us to jump. But there is in fact other evidence, not only from the sixteenth century but also from the fifteenth, and it shows that the notational peculiarity was not peculiar to Chamaterò alone, far from it. Consider, for instance, the following passage from the *Liber de arte contrapuncti* of Johannes Tinctoris, written in 1477. In this passage, Tinctoris gives a recommendation for what you should do if the cantus firmus is wildly leaping up and down—something that would rarely happen in plainchant, though his first example is actually written in plainchant neumes. If you are ever dealing with a cantus firmus like that, he says, then in your own counterpoint you should still aim to proceed in stepwise motion as much as possible. So in the first musical example, the cantus firmus, in void notes, leaps up and down like a deranged madman, but the counterpoint keeps its cool, and makes no leaps wider than the third. Here is how Tinctoris himself puts it.[23]

> Quarta regula est quod quam proximus et quam ordinatissimus poterit contrapunctus fieri debebit, etiam licet coniunctionibus longorum intervallorum tenor sic e converso formatus, ut hic patet:
>
> The fourth rule is that counterpoint must be fashioned as closely and as orderly as possible, even if the tenor, by contrast, is formed out of intervals of great size, as is shown here:

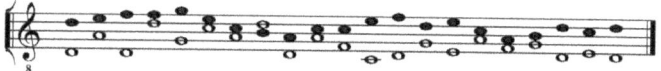

> Sed ab hac regula eximuntur, qui magis contrapuncto dulciori ac venustiori student quam propinquiori. Quique pluribus super librum

---

23. Johannes Tinctoris, *Liber de arte contrapuncti* (1477), III. iv. After Tinctoris, *Opera theoretica*, ed. Albert Seay, 2 vols., Corpus scriptorum de musica 22 (Rome: American Institute of Musicology, 1975–78), 2: 149.

canentibus ut contrapunctum diversificent, eum cum moderatione instar quodammodo compositorum longinquum efficiunt, ut hic patet:

Yet from this rule are exempted those who pursue a sweeter and more delightful counterpoint rather than a closer one, and who, with several singing on the book, introduce this wide leap in moderation, somewhat in the manner of composed songs, in order that they may diversify the counterpoint, as is shown here:

It is apparent from what Tinctoris says that the second example illustrates what you can hear when several musicians are singing upon the book, that is, improvising counterpoint upon a plainchant. And indeed, the lowest voice-part in the example moves in notes of equal value, as though this singer were also reading off the plainchant manuscript. The only difference is that Tinctoris does not notate that voice in the original neumes, but writes semibreves instead. Yet the implication is the same: when you are singing on the book, the plainchant is sung in notes of equal duration, and the other voices sing against the plainchant as though it were moving in semibreves.

So although Tinctoris and Chamaterò are almost a hundred years apart, there does seem to be some continuity between them. And this is indirectly confirmed in another passage of the same treatise by Tinctoris, when he discusses how you can sing counterpoint over a plainchant. Here, he gives us yet another example of *cantare super librum*, or *chanter sur le livre*, and it looks exactly as you might expect. Here is the passage.[24]

> Denique omnis contrapunctus aut super cantum planum aut figuratum fit. Super cantum planum quidem contrapunctum fieri contingit, quando ad voluntatem canentium quaelibet ipsius plani cantus nota una semibrevis minoris prolationis aut maioris tenetur, ut hic probatur:

> Lastly, all counterpoint is made either upon plainsong or figured song. It is indeed possible for counterpoint to be made upon a plainsong when those who are singing decide that every note of that plainsong be taken as one semibreve of major or minor prolation, as demonstrated here:

---

24. Tinctoris, *Liber de arte contrapuncti* (1477), II. xxi; after Tinctoris, *Opera theoretica*, 2: 110.

Tinctoris is being very circumspect here. He does not say that the plainchant is notated in semibreves, or even sung in semibreves, but that the other voices decide that its notes are to be taken as semibreves. The neumes are respected, the dignity and gravity of the plainchant is kept intact—even though, once again, the cantus firmus is notated in semibreves rather than neumes. Tinctoris also mentions other possibilities, like singing against the plainchant notes as though they were breves, or other note values. And he also mentions the most difficult of all possibilities, a plainchant that is genuinely unmeasured, in that no note need be of precisely the same duration as the next. Here is how he continues:

> ... In pluribus etiam ecclesiis cantus ipse planus absque mensura canitur, super quem suavissimus concentus ab eruditis efficitur. Et in hoc auris bona concinentibus necessaria est ut attentissime cursum tenoristarum animadvertant ne istis unam notam canentibus illi super aliam concinant.
>
> ... And in many churches this plainsong is sung without measure, upon which a most sweet concord is fashioned by expert singers. In this, it is necessary for the singers to have a good ear, in order that they may follow most attentively how the tenorists are progressing, lest, while these are singing one note, they are concording with another.

Of this kind of counterpoint, alas, he provides no example, though had he done so, he clearly would have been forced to notate the cantus firmus in plainchant neumes.

So there does appear to be a great deal of consistency here. When you sing *contraponto all'improvviso*, or when you are singing upon the book, it seems to be a well-established custom to sing the plainchant in notes of equal duration, notes that the other singers will typically interpret as semibreves. It is true that Tinctoris does not notate the cantus firmus in plainchant neumes. But just this notational peculiarity, polyphony with one voice written in neumes, is one that we find in choirbooks throughout Europe in the fifteenth and sixteenth centuries, usually in anonymous liturgical polyphony, usually in four voices, and usually in a fairly unassuming contrapuntal style. In my own research I am most familiar with it in German and Central European sources, like the Trent manuscripts, or the codex Specialnik, or Munich 3154 and Berlin 40021. Typically you see four voice-parts written out separately, of which three are in white mensural notation, and the fourth in plainchant notes. But it was certainly not an exclusively German or Italian tradition. In Appendix 2 I have printed a transcription of an anonymous four-part setting in the Gyffard Partbooks, copied in England in the 1550s. You will immediately recognize the same pattern: the cantus firmus moves in semibreves, which is the editor's interpretation of what were originally plainchant neumes. So here is an anonymous composer, certainly not familiar with anything happening in Italy, who writes down his composition in exactly the same way as Chamaterò, with the cantus firmus in plainchant notation. The setting itself, interestingly, is an Introit, for the Mass of Ascension Day, just like the settings of Chamaterò. So far as we know, the anonymous composer did not write it down in order to make a theoretical point about improvisation, or to present it to somebody as an illustration of what he and his fellow-singers were capable of doing. But it looks as if this might be a relic of the very tradition of contrapuntal improvisation that had died out four decades later, when Thomas Morley wrote his *Plaine and Easie Introduction*, and was no longer able to imagine that counterpoint could be sung this way.

It would be easy to spend the rest of this contribution giving other examples of this practice, which has no name, and which I have chosen to call, purely for my own reference, *cantus planus* settings, collected from all over Europe, in manuscripts from the fifteenth and sixteenth centuries. There are hundreds and hundreds of such settings, most of them not even available in modern editions, and the tradition as such is as yet completely unstudied. But apparently it was a universal tradition, and for a long time, even after the Reformation, it continued to be practiced in Catholic countries.

Against this background it is easier to understand why Seth Calvisius, that German music theorist who was so interested in the Papal bull *Docta sanctorum patrum*, should have credited Pope

John XXII with having established the tradition of improvised counterpoint. Let us listen once again to how Calvisius put it:

> [Here] the Pope makes plainchant the foundation of the consonances that are to be added. Whence, without any doubt, no other kind of music would be born than extemporized counterpoint, or that harmony which is called "autoschediastic." That is to say, when those who have deeper voices sing the plainchant *simpliciter*, yet the others, who have higher voices, add consonances, octaves, fifths, and fourths, at will, without forethought—just as is the custom today among certain court singers in chapels and in certain monasteries, and among Papal singers. Still, the singers of whom Pope [John] speaks, being less well trained, mingled their consonances perhaps from notation.

For Calvisius, then, the distinctive feature of improvised counterpoint is that the plainchant is sung *simpliciter*, that the neumes remain *simplex*, that is, unbroken and unrhythmicized. The examples we have seen earlier bear that out. And it is precisely this distinctive feature whose origin Calvisius ascribes to the papal bull of John XXII. Of course, we know that the feature may be older than that. I have emphasized earlier that the old *organum purum* from the twelfth century also had a plainchant notated in the original neumes. But *organum purum* was barely practiced anymore by the early fourteenth century, and it alone cannot account for the efflorescence of improvised counterpoint in the late Middle Ages and Renaissance. On this point, I do think Seth Calvisius may be an especially authoritative witness, precisely because he knows the tradition of improvised counterpoint like we no longer do, and because he knows how essential is the principle of keeping the plainchant notes *simplex*.

6.

So, whether we can bring ourselves to believe it or not, improvised counterpoint really did sound like the examples we have seen in this contribution. Or perhaps we should put it a little more carefully. To those who were familiar with the tradition, improvised counterpoint did sound like the examples printed above. That is why they transcribed them the way they did. To us it need not necessarily have sounded that way, too. Nor would we necessarily have transcribed it the way they did.

There is one major divide that separates us from the tradition of improvised counterpoint, and it is a divide that has more to do with how we listen and think than with the objective reality of the music itself. Since we are no longer familiar with the tradition, our principal frame of reference is composed music. So when we deal with improvisation, we have no choice but to define it in terms of composition. Question: what is improvisation? Answer: it is everything that composition is not. The problem with this answer is not just that it is symptomatic of the divide I just mentioned, but that it sets us up to expect improvisation to be a certain kind of music. Then when we hear an improvisation, or something claimed to be an improvisation, like the examples printed in this essay, it is not quite what we expect, or are capable of believing.

Let me give an example. If we lived in a culture in which everyday communication was done only in sign language, and in which we reserved the organ of speech exclusively for the recitation of works of high literary merit, we would probably lose the ability to speak spontaneously. Whatever we might try to say in a verbal utterance would inevitably be measured against the standards of the literary works we were accustomed to recite. And it would fall hopelessly short. If we then came in contact with another culture where people actually spoke spontaneously, we would probably need a word for what was special about their way of speaking. What we would say, conceivably, is: their speaking is improvised. Of course that would have seemed quite incredible to us, because we had only one stylistic register with which to hear and appreciate speech, namely a bookish one, and it was the wrong register with which to hear improvisation. The critical register we needed, and that we did not have, was "colloquial" rather than "bookish." Evaluating speech, in large part, is a matter of recognizing which register is being used, and on this point we have an almost implausibly keen sensibility. There is the stylistic register, not only of colloquial English, but of the scholarly article, of the sleeve notes, of talking with my brother back in Holland, of addressing a police officer, of making light conversation over a drink, and we shift registers effortlessly.

Yet we cannot make a similar shift in register when listening to improvised counterpoint, and as a consequence, that implausibly keen sensibility is heightened unreasonably. We may well be far less inclined to be tolerant of errors in improvised counterpoint than we would be in the performance of composed music. When you hear, for example, a motet by Palestrina sung in church and some singer gets it wrong at one point, we still know what he was supposed to sing, and we know that he will get it right the next time. We might still think it was overall a good performance. But the same sort or error in an improvisation would not be entitled to such leniency. It would trigger the very tripwire we had set up in advance: is it actually possible to improvise counterpoint? It would confirm what we had assumed to begin with—that you cannot improvise without violating the rules of counterpoint again and again. And so the error would distract us, to a greater degree than the same error might have done in a performance of a Dufay motet. That motet we could actually hear as music.

The same could be argued about transcriptions of improvisation. To return to our earlier analogy, if we were equipped only to recite literary English, and if someone claimed he could improvise speech without planning or premeditation, all we would be listening for was the sorts of errors you would never see in a literary text. We would not be equipped with the register for colloquial English, in which you barely hear those errors, or even not at all—not because the errors are not there, but because you automatically correct them, because you know what the speaker meant to say, or how he meant to say it. If we transcribed colloquial English, we would certainly not write down those errors exactly as they had been made, but would correct them without realizing that we were doing so. For an error has no place on paper. That is why we occasionally need the word *sic* to confirm that we actually intend to leave an error uncorrected, or to stop others from correcting it. We do not think it is cheating to render a spoken, improvised text in immaculate English, to edit out all the errors, and to tidy it up with punctuation. For in a sense, we really do hear colloquial English as we would transcribe it. And that, undoubtedly, is how Chamaterò transcribed the improvisations that had been sung under his direction: he transcribed not just what was being sung, but also how a proper listener would have heard it. This is what we would have heard if we had been familiar with the tradition.

In a way it makes perfect sense to shift attention away from the musical notation, per se, to the way it is heard. Because hearing and listening are also a living practice, an oral tradition, you might say, and one that has been lost, too. It is true that we have no choice but to re-encounter the tradition through its written traces, but those traces cannot tell us the whole story. In a way they are meant to leave us incredulous, to make us feel that music could not possibly have been improvised this way. For it is that gap, that divide, that reminds us what we have lost, and by whose disappearance we may one day be able to tell if we have truly regained it.

APPENDIX I.

Introit *Resurrexi et adhuc tecum sum*, from the Mass for Easter Sunday, with *contraponti all'improuiso* as printed in Chamaterò di Negri, *Li introiti* (1574).

What is Counterpoint?

Rob C. Wegman

APPENDIX 2.

Anonymous, *Viri Galilei*, LonBL Add. 17802–5 (Gyffard Partbooks), 65. After David Mateer, ed., *The Gyffard Partbooks*, Early English Church Music, 48 (London: Stainer and Bell, 2007), 1: 261–266.

For Ludwig Holtmeier

"*EX CENTRO*" IMPROVISATION
SKETCHES FOR A THEORY OF SOUND PROGRESSIONS IN THE EARLY BAROQUE

Johannes Menke

I.
THE BAROQUE TURNING POINT

It is a commonplace idea that after 1600, everything in music changed completely. The Baroque era started with monody, figured bass, opera, the "affects" and so on, whilst old-fashioned polyphony remained the same; so goes the accepted cliché. One can create wonderful antipodes like *prima pratica* against *seconda pratica*, the good Monteverdi as opposed to the bad Artusi, and good advancement against bad conservatism. Of course, history is not so simple. Musical style has many aspects – form, sound, harmony, counterpoint, articulation, melody etc. – and not all of them changed at the same time. The basic principles for organizing sound progressions, which are valid for composition as well as for improvisation, had already been established in the 16th century and many did not change.

It is another common thought that the 17th century represents a transitional epoch. It lies between modality and tonality, between classic intervallic counterpoint (the *stile antico*) and the new harmonic counterpoint of the Baroque, and between vocal and instrumental polyphony.[1] In spite of the experimental

---

1. Susan McClary speaks about the "seventeenth-century-interregnum," whose memory was "expunged" by tonality of the Enlightenment epoch (Susan McClary, "Towards a History of Harmonic Tonality," in *Towards Tonality* (Leuven: Leuven University Press, 2007), 117). I am in total agreement with her on this point, but doubt whether the term *interregnum* is the most suitable one. The 17th century seems to be an interregnum if we look at it from the perspective of tonal ideology. If we try to understand it from its own point of view, it reveals its own logical system and becomes – if we preserve the picture – a long-lasting kingdom with its own laws.

character of many pieces, there existed a clear technique of composition and improvisation, which was founded on the roots of Renaissance polyphony.[2]

This paper will concentrate solely on the question of sound progression, to which the topic improvisation will be linked. The term "sound progression"[3] has been consciously chosen in favour of "chord progression"; until the 18th century, there seems not to have been a clear concept of the chord. The chord is above all a phenomenon of performance practice, and is therefore often called a "hand position" (*Griffe*).[4] Nevertheless, the concept of sound progression, defined by the contrapuntal relationship of the outer voices to one another is the basis for improvisation as well as for composition. Here, a very important change happened: the outer-voice setting, which had been well established in the 16th century, became prevalent. Rolf Dammann distinguishes the *con centro* sound structure of the Renaissance from the *ex centro* sound structure of the Baroque,[5] arguing that whilst the *con centro* structure was focussed around the tenor in the middle, with the other voices being imagined in relation to it, the *ex centro* structure was clearly founded upon the bass over which the soprano built the framework. Sometimes – as in the trio sonata – the upper voices even seem to fight against one another, with each one attempting to become the highest voice.[6] Thus the *ex centro* sound structure emphasizes the "surface" of music. The

---

2. The Renaissance also remains the point of orientation in the arts.
3. I should like to refer here to two important articles by Markus Jans, "Alle gegen Eine. Satzmodelle in Note-gegen-Note-Sätzen des 16. und 17. Jahrhunderts," in *Basler Jahrbuch für historische Musikpraxis* 10 (Winterthur: Amadeus-Verlag, 1987), 101–120; and "Modale „Harmonik". Beobachtungen und Fragen zur Logik der Klangverbindungen im 16. und frühen 17. Jahrhundert," in *Basler Jahrbuch für historische Musikpraxis* 16 (Winterthur: Amadeus-Verlag, 1993), 167-188.
4. Even at the end of the century, as in Georg Muffat, *Regulae Concentum Partiturae* (1699), Georg Muffat, *Regulae concentuum partiturae*, ed. by Bettina Hoffmann und Stefano Lorenzetti (Bologna – Roma: Associazione Clavicembalistica Bolognese, 1991), 1-bis.
5. Rolf Dammann, *Der Musikbegriff im deutschen Barock* (Laaber: Laaber-Verlag, 1995), 195.
6. This is the opposite of the typical crossing tenor and contratenor voices in the 15th century, where these voices seem to be fighting to become the lowest voice.

skeleton is not internal, like the tenor in the *con centro* structure, but has become visible on the exterior. Composition and improvisation both take the surface as a point of departure from which they can execute their designs.

Continuing the conception of Dammann, one could say that there is a "double code" in the Baroque setting: the composition is defined by counterpoint, which concerns the relationship of the outer voices to one another, and continuo, which shows the perspective from the bass.[7] This means that a dyadic structure of outer voices is expanded through a chordal structure. In the case of trio structure, the upper voice is complemented by a second melodic voice. Here, there is a relationship, but also a certain independence, between both "codes." This independence concerns practical performance, where an ensemble of continuo players improvises the inner chordal structure, which thus has the possibility of becoming very complex.

The priority of the outer voices in fact started in the 15th century, where a clear relationship between the cantus and the contratenor bassus can often be observed, above all in four-voice settings, in which the tenth is often preferred between the outer voices – presumably because of its sensual sweetness. Nevertheless, most theorists do not describe the priority of the outer voices, but rather a system of completing the composition by adding voices.[8] One important exception to this, of course, is the treatise *Libro llamodo Arte taner Fantasia* (1565) by the Dominican Thomas de Sancta Maria. Here, Thomas gives ten possibilities for "harmonizing" a scale and defines them according to the relationship between the outer voices. The fourth manner (*quarta manera*) consists of using tenths and twelfths, in other words with thirds and fifths between the soprano and the bass (without the octave).

---

7. This means that the continuo numbers act as a kind of harmonic analysis, helpful for the continuo players.
8. For example, the famous *tavola del contrapunto* in Pietro Aaron, *Toscanello in Musica* (Venice, 1539), reprinted in Kassel, Bärenreiter, *libro secondo*, cap. XXI (not paginated).

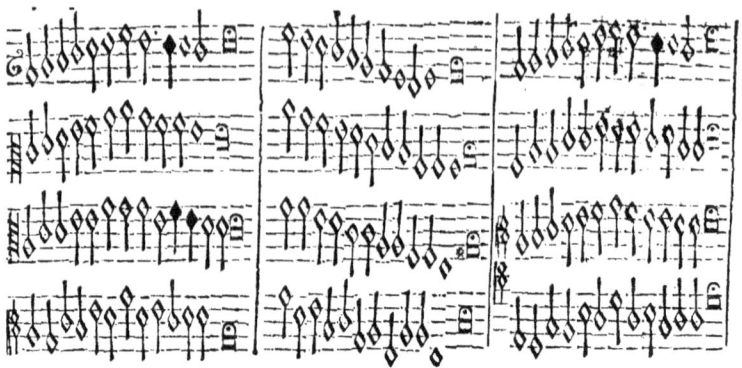

Example 1. Thomas de Sancta Maria, Libro llamodo Arte taner Fantasia *(1565)*, p. 22: *"La quarta manera se haze subiendo o baxando a dezenas y dozenas"*

Whereas these intervals are very often used in the fifteenth century between tenor and contratenor (combined with sixths or octaves between soprano and tenor), their alternation becomes a widely-used model for outer voices.

Example 2. *Use of alternating thirds and fifths between tenor and contratenor,* Gilles Binchois: Se la belle *(bars 5-11)*

The *con centro* 3-5 structure then becomes an *ex centro* one. One can find these 3-5 settings in the *Cancionero musical de Palacio* (1505-1525) as well as in Giulio Caccini's collection *Le nuove musiche* (1601/1614).

Example 3. Giulio Caccini (~1550-1618), 'Tu ch'hai le penne', *from:* Le nuove musiche II *(1614)*

Example 4. Juan del Encina (1469-1529), 'Si abrá en este baldrés', *from:* Cancionero musical de Palacio *(1505-1525), outer voices*

One advantage of the 3-5 setting is that the octave is reserved for the beginning and ending, so that the cadence is a real *perfectio* (3-5-8). Harmonizing a given melody, one can easily find a solution that also has thirds and fifths between the outer voices if the melody moves in leaps as well as in steps, as the following example will demonstrate:

Example 5. Bass to a given melody with alternating thirds and fifths: O Heiland, reiß die Himmel auf, *Friedrich Spee, 1622 (Augsburg, 1666)*

The third middle voice can now proceed in parallel thirds with the soprano, or can alternate between thirds and fifths.

Using this simple method, the composer or improviser is quickly able to find a "harmonization" that sounds convincing, without thinking about "tonality," or degrees of the scale, etc.[9]

2.
SKELETON AND DIMINUTION

One of the fundamental aspects of Western composition is the differentiation of a note-against-note framework and its diminution, that is to say the differentiation of a *contrapunctus simplex* and a *contrapunctus floridus*. In the second half of the 16th century, diminution seems to have become more and more important for the performer, as can be seen in the treatises of Thomas de Sancta Maria and Diego Ortiz. The thinking in stylistic patterns with which the progressions of the *contrapunctus simplex* could be embellished also remained into the 17th century, although the style changed. Comparing the diminution models of Thomas de Sancta Maria (in his *Libro Llamado Arte de Tañer Fantasia* [1565]) and Francesco Rognoni (in his *Selva de varii Passaggi* [Milan,

---

9. The famous "Tabula naturalis" of Johann Andreas Herbst also prefers the setting with thirds and fifths between bass and soprano (see *Musica poëtica*, [Nuremberg, 1643], 35-36).

1620]), the stylistic change is clearly perceptible: Rognoni uses more extensive passages and typical Baroque ornamental dissonances which Christoph Bernhard described as *superjectio, anticipatio, subsumtio* etc.[10] These models can be used in composition as well as in improvisation. In the well-known "aria" in the third act of his *Orfeo* (1607), Monteverdi provides a proposal for ornamentation. In this scene, Orfeo wants to persuade Caronte to give him back Euridice. For this purpose, Orfeo utilises all his skills and sings – following Monteverdi's proposal – a very *ex centro* embellished melody over an ostinato bass, which is based on the *Passamezzo* model (indicated by stars). The following example shows the dyadic outer-voice skeleton (without the ritornellos) together with an analysis of the intervals used (the last verse, which is similar to the fourth, has been omitted).

Monteverdi clearly prefers a 3-5 setting. This evokes the image of an improvising singer, who gravitates towards the 3-5 structure and fills it out with his own expressive and *ex centro* melodies. Octaves are almost entirely reserved for cadences. In the third verse, in which Orfeo says he will depart through the dark air *(cammin per l'aer cieco)*, Monteverdi's exclusive use of fifths is noteworthy. When Orfeo declares that he will reach paradise if he sees her beauty again *(Ch'ovunque stasis tanta bellezza il paradise ha seco)*, Monteverdi allows him to go up to a high F (in the embellished version) and down to a B natural. This shows that even such a simple and model-like skeleton is able to express the meaning of the text. The chromatic passage at the end of the fifth verse also relates to the text *(Ahi, chi niega il conforto a le mie pene?* [Ah, who can deny me comfort in my torment?]*)* and is also constructed as a 3-5 setting, using a third and then a fifth over

---

10. Christoph Bernhard, *Tractatus compositionis augmentatus*, in *Die Kompositionslehre Heinrich Schützens in der Fassung seines Schülers Christoph Bernhard*, ed. Joseph Müller-Blattau (Kassel: Bärenreiter, 1963). The title of this German edition, which was first printed in 1926, is symptomatic of the ideology of "the great German composers." Instead of describing the technique of Schütz, Bernhard in fact describes the technique of Italian composers, which he learned during his journey to Italy. There, he studied with Giacomo Carissimi, who was probably a more important model for Bernhard than Schütz.

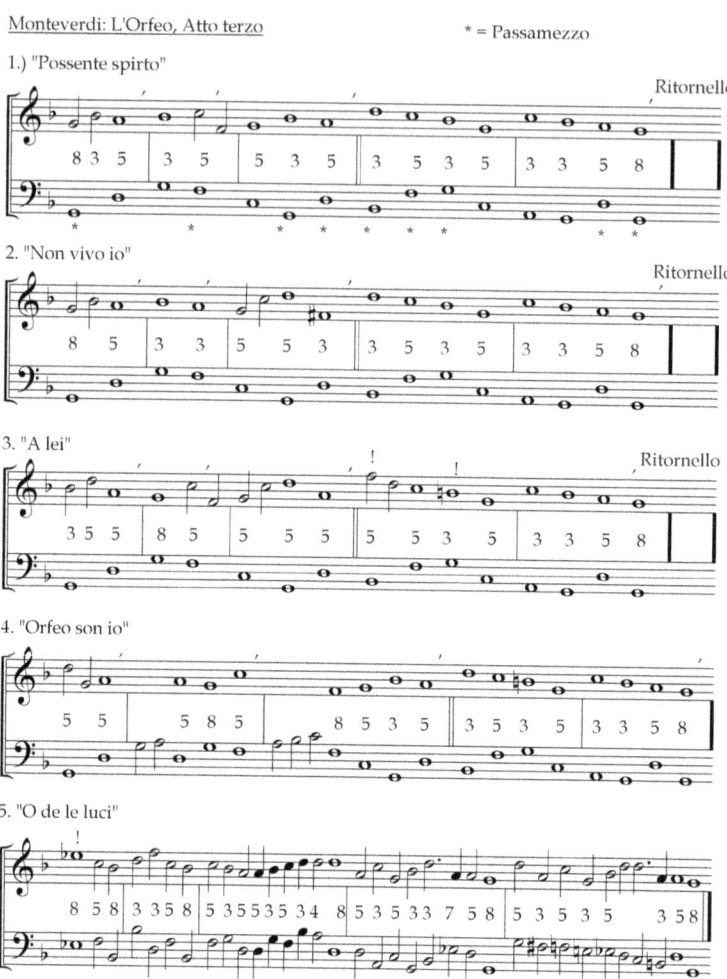

Example 6. Monteverdi: Orfeo, *Act III. Outer-voice-reduction of Orfeo's aria*

the descending semitones in the bass. The continuo player has to play sixth chords above the F sharp and the E sharp in order to avoid diminished fifths. In any case, the 3-5 setting can also be used in chromatic situations.

3.
COMBINATORIAL THINKING

Although the 3-5 setting produces satisfying sound progressions, it was not the only principle used. Its popularity was due to the fact that it allowed octaves to be reserved for cadences and also prevented problems with parallels.

The following diagram from Giovanni Maria Artusi's *L'arte del contrapunto* (Venice 1586, p.18), which was adopted by other authors (for instance Bartolomeo Bismatova in his *Compendio musicale* [Ferrara, 1677], p.42), was the first of its kind to demonstrate the thought-out possibilities. It is possible to connect perfect and imperfect consonances in four ways: P-P, P-I, I-P, I-I.

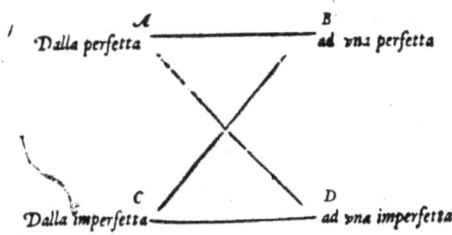

Example 7. Giovanni Maria Artusi: "i movimenti delle Consonanze"

Because all progressions are reversible, it is not really necessary to distinguish P-I and I-P. Taking concrete intervals and avoiding mistakes like 5-5, the following interval progressions exist:

P-P	5-8
I-P	3-5, 3-8, *6-5, 6-8,*
I-I	3-3, *6-6, 3-6*

Coming from another perspective, namely that of the three types of contrapuntal motion, the following possibilities are available:

	Motus rectus	Motus contrarius	Motus obliquus
P-P	5-8	5-8	5-8
I-P	3-5, *6-5*	3-5, 3(10)-8, *6-8,*	3-5, *5-6, 6-8,* 3(10)-8
I-I	3-3, *6-6*	3-3(10), *3-6*	*3-6*

Of course, this overview gives no indication as to the quality of the progressions. Some of them, like the 3-5 setting, are standard whilst others are not, but they are all possible, and were all in fact used. Harmonically, the 6ths will become sixth chords, and are therefore printed cursively. A further step would be to distinguish stepwise motion (*per grado*) from motion in leaps (*per salto*). It is perhaps important to know that in stepwise motion, which melodically speaking is, of course, preferred, only certain possibilities exist:

	Motus rectus	Motus contrarius	Motus obliquus
P-P	-	-	-
I-P	-	3-5, 10-8, *6-8*	*5-6*
I-I	3-3, *6-6*	-	-

Using leaps, however, each *motus* and each interval connection will work in several combinations.

With the establishment of basso continuo as the norm, the organization of composition was built upon the principle of the bass as a primary voice. Looking at the bass, which represents the "ground plan" of the composition, the performance is led by the continuo player. Yet in 1607, the matter seems to be absolutely clear for the theorist Francesco Bianciardi, who writes:

> Principalmente si considerano i movimenti del Baßo come fondamento della musica, che procede da una corda all'altra, salendo in cinque modi, e descendendo in altri cinque, come nell' eßempio.

Firstly, the movements of the bass are considered as a fundamental element of music which moves from one note ("corda") to the other, rising in five ways and descending in another five, as in the example.[11]

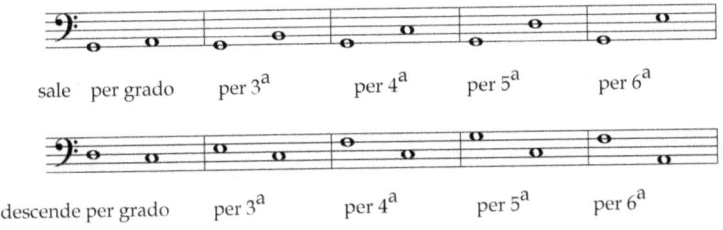

Example 8. „I movimenti del basso" in Franceso Bianciardi

This clear system now acts as the framework for the organization of sound progressions, it being employed in the bass voice with the possible sound structures being placed upon it. During the 17th century, it became usual to build sequences using these *movimenti*.[12] One of the most significant treatises is undoubtedly the *Nova Instructio* by Johann Nenning, called "Spiridionis", from 1670.[13]

He names his bass progressions *cadentiae*, a term which has nothing to do with the cadence as a syntactic formula. For each *cadentia*, he sometimes supplies more than 100 possibilities of different diminutions and upper voices. His order of *cadentiae* is as follows:

---

11. Franceso Bianciardi, *Breve Regola per imparar'a sonare sopra il Basso con ogni sorte d'Instrumento* (Siena 1607).
12. See Johannes Menke, "Historisch-systematische Überlegungen zur Sequenz seit 1600," in *musik.theorien der gegenwart 3*, ed. Clemens Gadenstätter and Christian Utz (Saarbrücken: Pfau 2008), 87-111.
13. In two volumes, edited by Eduardo Bellotti (Colledara: Andromeda, 2003 and Latina: Il Levante, 2008).

INDEX TOTIUS OPERIS

Mille Variationes supra:

Example 9. Spiridion, Nova Instructio, vol II, p. XXII

Taking one of these models, namely that of descending thirds (third line on the right), one could try to use all of the interval combinations so far discussed: P-P (5-8), I-P (3-5, 3-8, 6-5, 6-8) and I-I (3-3, 6-6, 3-6).

Example 10. Possible upper voices of the sequence of descending thirds

Whilst these possibilities do not suit every style, it is nevertheless clear that they are effective realizations in themselves. The additional third voice should be incorporated in such a way as to fill out the perfect intervals with thirds. Of course, more than one added third voice is available in each case. It is clear that these added voices correspond to other possible upper voices. Each melody, which can also be a middle voice, is also a certain sequence, and in some cases is also the descending third sequence. This overview can therefore be seen as a kind of matrix of possibilities that can be combined. The more experience an improviser or a composer has, the more consciously he will be able to utilize these skeletons in different combinations and find different diminutions for them.

Spiridionis demonstrated this, not in a systematical way as has just been attempted above, but by enumeration. The following example shows the different outer voices used by Spiridionis without diminutions.

Example 11. Upper voices of the sequence of descending thirds used by Spiridionis[14]

He uses little more than 50% of all of the possibilities, and seems to choose at random. The task of theoreticians today is to unravel the implicit theory of practical treatises like that by Spiridionis, which seems to be based on "combinatorial" thinking and seeks to find possibilities. Were there enough space here, one could list examples from compositions of the 17th century for each possible melody.

---

14. Taken from Johannes Menke, "Historisch-systematische Überlegungen zur Sequenz seit 1600," in *musik.theorien der gegenwart 3*, ed. Clemens Gadenstätter and Christian Utz (Saarbrücken: Pfau 2008), 101.

4.
CLASSIFICATION OF CHORDS

In the early Baroque, however, the problem of the sixth chord became clearly-defined. Bianciardi describes the triad as the *armonia perfetta*, consisting of a perfect (fifth) and an imperfect (third) interval.[15] Further continuing Bianciardi's thinking, one could call the sixth chord an *armonia imperfetta* because it consists of two imperfect intervals. From this systematization, an analogy of chords and intervals could be developed:

	PERFECT	IMPERFECT	DISSONANT
Interval	8, 5	3, 6	2, 4, 7, 9
Chord	5	6	4 5 6 4 6 7 9…
	3	3	2, 2, 4, 3, 5, 5, 7…
Function	calm	motion	tension

Bianciardi relates the use of the sixth chord to the scale or, more exactly, to the hexachord: it has to be placed on the *mi*-degree, must be natural or made so by accidentals. Following this principle, we obtain a "rule of the octave" with sixth chords on the third and seventh degrees of the scale in the Lydian mode.[16] We cannot really use the term "major" and "minor" in the early 17th century, but they are not so far away because the Lydian (always with B flat), Mixolydian (mostly with the leading note) and Dorian (with the leading note and B flat, going down to the fifth degree) modes are almost used like major and minor. If in addition the sixth chord is used on a *tenorizans* cadence on the second and sixth degrees (which resolve onto the first and fifth degrees respectively), a crude version of the later rule of the octave becomes discernible. Nevertheless, it is important to stress that

---

15. Francesco Bianciardi, *Breve Regola per imparar'a sonare sopra il Basso con ogni sorte d'Instrumento* (Siena 1607).
16. See Markus Jans, "Towards a History of the Origin and Development of the Rule of the Octave," in *Towards Tonality* (Leuven: Leuven University Press, 2007), 119-143.

5.
OSTINATOS

So far, the 3-5 setting, "combinatorial" thinking, sequences and the scale-related use of sixth chords have been considered as categories for constructing sound progressions. Two very important categories must be included as well: ostinatos and dissonant sound progressions. A catalogue of ostinato patterns will not be included in this paper, but their enormous importance and widespread circulation cannot be overemphasised. It was fashionable to use them in compositions as well as in improvisations. Indeed, it would hardly be an exaggeration to say that the 17th century – particularly the first half – was the century of ostinatos. All ostinatos are related to a certain bass progression, but some of them, like the *Passacaglia* or *Chaconne*, only have fixed points and can be varied between these points in many ways. For our special interest, it is important that some of these ostinatos are connected with certain interval progressions in the outer voices, meaning that the ostinatos are defined differently. These could be categorised according to measure, mode, interval skeleton, bass progression, melody and character, but very few of these represent constitutive categories. For instance, the *Passamezzo antico* is defined by its mode (transposed "Dorian" in G) and by a certain bass progression (G-F-G-D/G[or B flat]-F-G-D-G), and can appear in different metres (as in the *Gagliarda* or *Pavana*) and can have different melodies. The *Romanesca*, however, is in the same mode and has a similar bass progression (B flat-F-G-D/B flat-F-G-D-G), but is always connected by a triple metre (which often is hidden in a duple-measure) and a 3-5 setting in the outer-voice skeleton.[17] This skeleton can sometimes be abandoned in variations but still always resonates through the composition. Thus 10

---

17. Nevertheless, the *Passamezzo* can also be realized as a 3-5 or an 8-3 setting, but must not do so unconditionally in order to be recognizable.

of the 14 variations of Girolamo Frescobaldi on the *Romanesca*, for example, begin with a third in the outer voices, clearly signalling the *Romanesca* opening. In contrast, the *Folia* (both the early and the later model) is used mostly in the untransposed D mode and is defined by an 8-3 setting in the outer voices.

a) Skeleton of the *Aria della Romanesca*

b) Skeleton of the early *Folia*

c) Skeleton of the *Aria di Folia*

Example 12. Outer voice-skeletons of arias

The 3-5 and 8-3 settings are connected to each other because the third voice in a 3-5 setting is an 8-3 setting and vice versa. If an ensemble is improvising a *Romanesca* or *Folia*, the players can agree beforehand who will take which of the two parts. During the variations they will change their roles.[18]

---

18. Still Antonio Vivaldi's *Sonata op. 1 RV 63* "La Follia" is a good example of this technique. Therefore, this piece is indeed a kind of written improvisation.

6.
DISSONANT PROGRESSIONS

Perhaps the most significant development regarding the construction of sound progressions was the increase of dissonant syncopations during the 16th century and the subsequent use of dissonant chords during the 17th and 18th centuries. In the compositions of Palestrina, which were judged as models for composition around and still after 1600, dissonant syncopation is omnipresent and has achieved some independence from the cadence, from which it actually originates. In this respect, Palestrina's music is not as conservative as is often supposed. It is known that theorists such as Vincenzo Galilei described some great liberties concerning the treatment of dissonances. To understand the historic development, it is perhaps more interesting to see which models actually became standard during the second half of the 16th century. Only three intervallic combinations, whose entire potential unfolded during the 17th century, will be emphasized here.

a) The consonant fourth inside a certain cadence formula, which Nicola Vicentino dubbed *sincopa tutta cattiva*.[19] Vicentino judges this formula to be *non [...] moderna*, maybe because it was used very often in the Frottola-repertoire around 1500. Yet despite Vicentino's opinion, this formula continued to be considered "modern." Its usage even increased, and it was a standard cadence formula (known in Italy as the *cadenza doppia*) until the 18th and early 19th centuries. In the 17th century, it became fashionable to use the *cadenza doppia*[20] in sequences (mostly in descending fifths or ascending seconds). Angelo Berardi in turn described this as *motivo di cadenza*.[21] Palestrina had already used such a sequence with a *cadenze doppie* at the beginning of the *Christe* in his *Missa*

---

19. See Nicola Vicentino, *L'antica musica ridotta alla moderna prattica* (Rome, 1555), 30. The formula was, of course, also described by other authors, for instance by Gioseffo Zarlino in his *Le Istitutioni harmoniche* (Venice, 1558), 246.
20. I personally prefer the term "*cadenza doppia*" because "*cadenza tutta cattiva*" (totally bad, means dissonant cadence) is a very negative description.
21. Angelo Berardi, *Documenti armonici*, (Bologna, 1687), in Andrea Bornstein's edition, http://www.musica-antica.info/berardi/.

Nasce la gioja mia. Formulas like this cadential model were, of course, welcome material for improvisations, where they can be combined and ornamented to great effect.

The *Cadenza tutta cattiva/cadenza doppia* obviously produces new cadential formulae in the upper voices. Ludwig Holtmeier has proposed calling these formulae as *doppia-soprano-clause* and *doppia-tenor-clause*:[22] there exist two versions of the *doppia-tenor* because it can be extended by a syncopated seventh.

Example 13. Clauses of the cadenza doppia

These two cadential formulae can now become *ex centro*. That means they can appear on the surface, namely in the outer voices. If one does this, the outer voices obviously become linear. By taking a linear bass and combining it with the cadential formulae of the other voices, one indeed achieves a complete example of the rule of the octave:[23]

Example 14[24]: *Rule of the octave as combination of cadenze doppie*

---

22. See Ludwig Holtmeier, "Zum Tonalitätsbegriff der Oktavregel, " in *Systeme der Musiktheorie*, ed. Clemens Kühn and John Leigh (Dresden: Sandstein, 2009), 13-15.
23. See also Holtmeier, 14.
24. Taken from Ludwig Holtmeier, Johannes Menke, Felix Diergarten, eds., *Giovanni Paisiello: Regole per bene accompagnare il partimento o sia il basso sopra il Cembalo* (Wilhelmshaven: Noetzel, 2008), 152.

Thus the "antique" (according to Vicentino) *cadenza tutta cattiva* has enormous potential if it is used in an *ex centro* way.[25]

b) In addition, two new resolutions of the fourth are a consequence of *ex centro* middle voices. Normally, the upper note of the fourth has to be treated as a dissonance. During the 16th century, two other resolutions were established in which the lower voice was resolved as a dissonance, going to a diminished fifth or into a sixth. One can interpret this new resolution as a kind of *ex centro* development which has his origin in the so-called "semiperfect cadence." In the next example we can see first a cadence with a tenor-clausula in the bass, which Gallus Dressler called "semiperfect"[26] (a), then the upper voices as outer voices, producing a 2-4-[6]-chord (b) and two other versions of the same bass with changed upper voices.

Example 15. Ex centro-versions of the semiperfect cadence

Many of the advanced dissonance resolutions around 1600 work with the diminished fifth and the augmented fourth. The diminished fifth can be used as dissonance as well as resolution. The following example shows advanced resolutions from Giovanni Maria Artusis *L'arte del contraponto* (Bologna 1598) in an *ex centro* manner, namely as outer voices with added thorough-bass figures (which one can of course not find in Artusi). Some of them Christoph Bernhard will describe later as *syncopatio catachrestica*.

---

25. Johannes Menke, "Die Familie der candenza doppia," *Zeitschrift der Gesellschaft für Musiktheorie*, http://www.gmth.de/zeitschrift/artikel/654.aspx.
26. See Robert Forgàcs, *Gallus Dressler's Praecepta musicae poeticae* (Chicago: University of Illinois Press, 2007), 147-149.

"Ex Centro" Improvisation

Example 16. Advanced resolutions by Artusi used as outer voices

In all examples it is possible to change the outer voices. Doing this, we get some resolutions which are typical "baroque". The following example shows three cadence-resolutions, which have its origin in the 16th century. In the 17th century we find versions of them with changed outer voices (second system) and even versions, where a V-I bass is added below (third system). The second example of the third system shows the framework of a typical baroque French cadence, the last example, in which a ninth is resolved into a seventh is a standard in trio sonatas by Corelli.

Example 17. Advanced cadential resolutions with changed voices and added basses

7.
CONCLUSION: *EX CENTRO* IMPROVISATION

To summarize: there were not different sets of rules for improvisation and composition during the 16th and 17th centuries. But there was an unfolding of possibilities in the early Baroque. To understand the technique of improvisation, one must understand the principles of compositional technique in general. The key to understanding this lies in the concept of sound progressions, already established in the 16th century and, as skeletons, the basis for composition as well as improvisation, *ex centro* thinking. Since other qualities of Baroque music were also *ex centro*, it would be worth concluding by reviewing the different aspects which define *ex centro*:

- The sound structure is *ex centro* when one takes the outer voice as a constitutive skeleton.
- Finding as many variants as possible has an *ex centro* quality (for a skeleton or for a diminution, see Spiridionis!).
- Compared with the 16th century, the style of diminution has become *ex centro*. More and more ornamental diminution becomes a part of composition.
- The representation of "affects" is *ex centro* because the musical structure is always a consequence of the "affects" which are to be represented.
- The unfolding of infinite variations over relatively simple *ostinato* patterns is an *ex centro* activity.
- Dissonances are used in an *ex centro* way: firstly, by being used very frequently; secondly, by building dissonant chords; and thirdly, by establishing new resolutions.
- Original middle voices are treated as *ex centro* outer voices. They can be changed and new basses can be added to them. This combinatoriality produces new treatment of dissonances, as well as new standard progressions.

The roots of all of these developments lie in the late 16th century. Evolving towards the Baroque era, the composer, as well as the improviser, moves more and more in an *ex centro* fashion on the surface of music, and this surface is then to become the stage for a genuinely Baroque musical theatre. In his famous chapter "Von den Theatralischen Resolutionibus der Dissonantien" in his treatise 'Der Generalbass in der Composition' (Dresden 1728, p. 585 following) Johann David Heinichen unfolds many further possibilities, but this has to be examined in another article.

FROM IMPROVISATION TO COMPOSITION: THREE 16TH CENTURY CASE STUDIES[1]

Peter Schubert

Having learned these types [of interval] and the method, here is how we ought to use them: The boy provides himself with a slate on which one may write and erase; he takes a Tenor from plainchant and at first writes note against note, using these types. Whenever he has gotten used to making note against note by improvisation and has become practiced in it, then he can go on to florid counterpoint. In this, when he has become trained, he will put aside the slate and learn to sing in improvising on a plainchant or on figured music printed in a book or copied on a sheet of paper.[2]

Although it is well known that improvisation played an important role in Renaissance musical life, the details of this polymorphous practice in the sixteenth century have not been sufficiently investigated. There are many angles from which to look at improvisation: Anna Maria Busse Berger has written about the importance of memory and visualization in music up through the 15th century; Ross Duffin has done hands-on experiments in

---

1. A version of this paper was presented at the Orpheus Institute in Ghent on April 7 & 9, 2009, including demonstrations of improvised counterpoint using *contraponto fugato*, three parts with two in parallel tenths, two parts invertible at the twelfth, and three parts in *stretto fuga*. The author wishes to thank his co-improvisers Catherine Motuz and Steven Vande Moortele, as well as Julie Cumming, Rodolfo Moreno, Jane Hatter, Marta Albala, Jacob Sagrans, Duncan Schouten, and Alison Laywine for their advice and assistance.
2. Adrianus Petit Coclico, *Compendium musices* (Nuremberg: Montanus and Neuber, 1552; facs. Kassel: Bärenreiter, 1954), trans. Albert Seay as *Musical Compendium* (Colorado Springs: Colorado College Music Press, 1973), 22-23. Another author who proposes writing as a means of learning improvisation is Hothby. See Benjamin Brand, "A Medieval *Scholasticus* and Renaissance Choirmaster: A Portrait of John Hothby at Lucca," *Renaissance Quarterly* lxii/3 (2010): 754-806. Hothby says "…by composing you will learn how to sing discant, which is what you want to know at present…" p. 783.

15th century improvisation; Richard Sherr, Timothy McGee, Tim Carter, Rob Wegman and Jane Flynn have looked at its social and liturgical functions in the 16th century; Klaus-Jürgens Sachs has made a sweeping survey of types of improvised counterpoint through the Renaissance;[3] Philippe Canguilhem has made a thorough study of Lusitano's massive treatise on improvisation;[4] Folker Froebe has looked at 16th century improvisation as a harbinger of harmonic sequence;[5] and most recently Barnabé Janin has published a textbook for improvisation based on the practical experience of Jean-Yves Haymoz.[6]

None of these authors has systematically investigated or tried out the veritable explosion of contrapuntal techniques that are described in 16th century treatises. I have elsewhere given a

---

3. Among more recent studies, see Anna Maria Busse Berger and Massimiliano Rossi, ed., *Memory and Invention: Medieval and Renaissance Literature, Art and Music* (Florence: Leo S. Olschki, 2009); Anna Maria Busse Berger, "The Problem of Diminished Counterpoint," in *Uno gentile et subtile ingenio: Studies in Renaissance Music in Honour of Bonnie J. Blackburn*, ed. Gioa Filocamo and M. Jennifer Bloxam (Turnhout: Brepols, 2009), 13-27; Ross Duffin, "*Contrapunctus Simplex et Diminutus*: Polyphonic Improvisation for Voices in the Fifteenth Century," *Basler Jahrbuch für historische Musikpraxis* (2007): 73-94; Tim Carter, "'Improvised' Counterpoint in Monteverdi's 1610 Vespers," in *Uno gentile et subtile ingenio: Studies in Renaissance Music in Honour of Bonnie J. Blackburn*, ed. Gioa Filocamo and M. Jennifer Bloxam (Turnhout: Brepols, 2009), 29-35; Jane Flynn, "The education of choristers in England during the sixteenth century," in *English choral practice c.1400–c.1650: A memorial volume to Peter Le Huray*, John Morehen, ed. (Cambridge: Cambridge University Press, 1995), 180-199; Timothy McGee, "*Cantare all'improvviso*: Improvising to poetry in late Medieval Italy," in *Improvisation in the arts of the Middle Ages and Renaissance*, Timothy McGee, ed. (Kalamazoo: Western Michigan University, 2003), 31-70; Klaus-Jürgen Sachs, "Arten improvisierter Mehrstimmigkeit nach Lehrtexten des 14. bis 16. Jahrhunderts," *Basler Jahrbuch für historische Musikpraxis* 7 (1983): 166-183; Richard Sherr, "The Singers of the *Papal Chapel* and Liturgical Ceremonies in the Early Sixteenth Century: Some Documentary Evidence," in *Rome in the Renaissance, the City and Myth*, ed. P.A. Ramsey, Medieval and Renaissance Texts and Studies 18 (Binghamton, NY: 1982), 249-264.
4. See P. Canguilhem, *Chanter sur le livre à la Renaissance: Les traités de contrepoint de Vicente Lusitano* (Turnhout: Brepols, 2013).
5. Folker Froebe, "Satzmodelle des Contrapunto alla mente und ihre Bedeutung für den Stilwandel um 1600," *Zeitschrift der Gesellschaft für Musiktheorie* 4 (2007): 13-55. http://www.gmth.de/zeitschrift/artikel/244.aspx
6. Barnabé Janin, *Chanter sur le livre, Manuel pratique d'improvisation polyphonique de la Renaissance*, (Langres: Dominique Guéniot, 2012).

bird's-eye view of these techniques and shown that the very term "counterpoint" referred to improvisation.[7]

In Part I of this essay, I will attempt a comprehensive list of what could be improvised and look closely at four techniques that show up often in repertoire; in Part II, I will elaborate the distinction between improvisation and composition as it appears in three treatises.

I will show that singers could improvise more sophisticated structures than we expect (even Zarlino is amazed at the *ex tempore* skills he describes), and contrast these skills with what seems to be implied by the word "composition." Drawing primarily on the writings of Coclico, Pontio, and Morley, I will demonstrate how Renaissance musicians in the second half of the sixteenth century may have improvised, how they conceived the difference between improvisation and composition, and how our knowledge of improvised practices can affect our conception of compositional process. One of the most interesting by-products of this study is that melodic material, the theme, both determines and is determined by the use to which it will be put—i.e., how the melody influences a contrapuntal *inventio* before it is deployed formally (in the phase of *dispositio*).[8]

---

7. Peter Schubert, "Counterpoint pedagogy in the Renaissance," in *The Cambridge history of Western music theory*, ed. Thomas Christensen (Cambridge: Cambridge University Press, 2002), 503-533. See also "From Voice to Keyboard: Improvised Techniques in the Renaissance." *Philomusica on-line* [http://philomusica.unipv.it] 11/1(2012): 11-22.

8. For Pontio, the word *inventione* applied to a melodic motive and a contrapuntal combination. See Russell Murray, "The Theorist as Critical Listener: Pietro Pontio's Nine *Case di Varietà*," *Theoria* 10 (2003): 19-58.

I.
WHAT COULD BE IMPROVISED?

Two-Part Improvisation
1. Adding a single line to a CF in even note values or in mixed note values
    a. in note-against-note texture (includes gymel)
    b. in mixed values or in species
    c. with a fresh repeating motive (contraponto fugato) or with a repeating motive derived from the chant (ad imitatione), or with the motive inverted
    d. any of the above that makes an invertible combination (includes "mirror" inversion)

2. Singing or playing in two-part stretto fuga

Three- and Four-Part Improvisation
3. Adding multiple lines to a CF in even note values or in mixed note values
    a. adding two lines in fauxbourdon
    b. adding two lines, one in parallel tenths
    c. adding two lines in canon with each other
    d. adding three lines (in contraponto fugato, in falsobordoni, also called the "parallel-sixth model," or in various interval patterns against a scale)

4. Adding a line to a pre-existing duo

5. Singing or playing in 3- or 4-vv. stretto fuga *(doppia consequenza)*

Example 1. Improvised techniques found described in various treatises

Example 1 shows a list of improvised techniques found in various treatises. Many have been discussed elsewhere,[9] and for reasons of space, I will focus on the four that I have practiced: 1c, *contraponto fugato* (or *ad imitatione*) in two parts; 1d, invertible counterpoint in two parts; 3c, adding two lines in canon to a CF; and 2 and 5, stretto fuga in 2-3 parts. I will propose some scenarios for their use, investigate some practical problems in their application, and illustrate how these techniques show up in examples from composed repertoire.

Contrapunto Fugato

This is perhaps the most important to many different types of composition. All cantus firmus (CF) compositions use this technique, and even in two-part music it can build simple musical forms.[10] I have cited many authors on this subject[11] and described its use in a textbook, *Modal Counterpoint, Renaissance Style*.[12] Banchieri's little motet on *ecce sacerdos magnus* (Example 2) is a good example

---

9. This list may profitably be compared to the "Twenty Tests for Applicants for the Post of Choirmaster at Toledo Cathedral in 1604," reprinted in Philippe Canguilhem "Singing upon the book according to Vicente Lusitano," *Early Music History* 30 (2011): 102-103. See discussions of fauxbourdon, gymel and parallel sixths and parallel tenths by Johannes Menke in this volume. See also Markus Jans "Alle gegen Eine: Satzmodelle in Note-gegen-Note-Sätzen des 16. und 17. Jahrhunderts," *Basler Jahrbuch für historische Musikpraxis* 10 (1986): 101-120 and Peter Schubert, *Modal Counterpoint, Renaissance Style*, 2nd ed. (New York: Oxford University Press, 2008), 192-194. Adding a line to a duo has not been discussed in recent research, and it is difficult to imagine how this was done: was the piece scored up, or did the improviser look at two separate parts?
10. The Ortiz ricercars are excellent examples of the technique (see Peter Schubert, *Modal Counterpoint, Renaissance Style*, 2nd ed. (New York: Oxford University Press, 2008), ex. 9-15), with long segments repeated in the added voice. Lusitano recommends a kind of ABA form using the repeating motive. See Henri Collet, ed., *Un tratado de canto de organo (siglo XV): Manuscrito en la Biblioteca Nacional de Paris* (Ph.D. diss., Université de Paris, 1913), p. 76 and ex. 50. For more on Lusitano, see Philippe Canguilhem, "Singing upon the Book According to Vicente Lusitano," *Early Music History* 30 (2011): 55-103.
11. Peter Schubert, "Counterpoint pedagogy in the Renaissance," in *The Cambridge history of Western music theory*, ed. Thomas Christensen (Cambridge: Cambridge University Press, 2002), 510-514.
12. Peter Schubert, *Modal Counterpoint, Renaissance Style*, 2nd ed. (New York: Oxford University Press, 2008), chs. 8 and 9, and appendix 4.

of what a young singer might have improvised, beginning with *contraponto ad imitatione* (the motive is borrowed from the first five notes of the chant), then moving on to repeat various freely invented motives.[13] The end of this example is particularly effective and well formed, with short sequential repetitions of *et inventus est justus*, the last of which is extended into the cadence.

Example 2. Banchieri Cartella, p. 67

In *Modal Counterpoint* I proposed an easy way to learn to do this: begin with the short motive (*passo*) and memorize all possible CF motions that could support that motive.[14] I have done this myself,

---

13. Adriano Banchieri, *Cartella musicale* (Venice: G. Vincenti, 1614; facs. Bologna: Forni, 1983), 67.
14. Peter Schubert, *Modal Counterpoint, Renaissance Style*, 2nd ed. (New York: Oxford University Press, 2008), 115-116.

but it is very limiting, and it is unlikely that a singer, faced with a new CF, would have come to church with a particular motive ready to go.[15] More likely, he would find ("invent") a possible motive over the first notes of the chant (possibly influenced by the words he had to sing, or by the CF itself as in the Banchieri example), and then look ahead for opportunities to use it.

That process is illustrated in one of the contemporaneously transcribed multi-part improvisations discussed by Rob Wegman (see Example 3).[16] I believe that the tenor, who started the improvisation, noticed that the first five CF notes, F-E-F-G-F, are repeated in notes 7-11; he invented an eight-note figure beginning with a syncopated semibreve and two descending steps (#1) that could be executed over both CF fragments. As CF notes 3-4 could support the first three notes of that same line, the quintus can sound that motive (#1), as long as the tenor gets out of the way. The tenor then takes the next opportunity to sound the whole figure in its entirety beginning in m. 4, and the cantus sounds the fragment of motive #1 that the quintus had sung in m. 2. This is only possible if the quintus foregoes that opportunity, making way for the cantus singer to do it. In the second measure, the cantus introduces a different figure (#2) over F-G, ending with an ascending *tirata* D-A; the altus waits until F-G comes back (notes 9-10 in the CF) and repeats what the cantus did, the cantus having gotten out of the way.[17] The result of all this is that mm. 2 and 5 contain the same four-voice combination, or module, albeit with some motives sung by other singers, some in different registers.

---

15. Peter Schubert, "Composing Without a Score ca. 1600" (paper presented at the annual meeting of the Society for Music Theory, Atlanta, GA, November 13, 1999). In a recent workshop on improvisation, students were taught only one motive at first, and encouraged to place it only against stepwise motions of the CF. However, they had to know what note they were singing and what interval above the CF was sounding in order to know if the motive could be placed over a given step, both of which are challenging to present-day singers. From these humble beginnings quite respectable counterpoints grew (www.mentemani.org/Connection/Phase_Two.html).

16. The example, from *Li introiti fondati sopra il canto fermo del basso* by Hippolito Chamaterò di Negri (Venice: l'herede di Girolamo Scotto, 1574) is transcribed by Rob C. Wegman in "What is Counterpoint?," this volume.

17. Motives #1 and #2 both begin "fa-mi" as the CF does, and so are both examples of *contraponto ad imitatione*.

Example 3. (Chiamaterò di Negri)

Chamaterò di Negri's example illustrates some of Pontio's precepts for singing in counterpoint: rests hardly ever occur and cadences are rare.[18] Pontio, however, does allow cadences when a motive (*inventione*) is repeated or when a new one is introduced, and we can see this at the cadence to F in bar 11, where various ascending *tirate* (#3 and others) are repeated more frequently, and at the cadence to G in bar 17, which is followed by a new motive (#4) in m. 18. (Motives 1-4 are the longest or most often repeated; other shorter or fragmentary motives have not been labeled.)

We might share Morley's famous skepticism about several singers doing ensemble improvisation;[19] but Juan Bermudo reports hearing impressive demonstrations: "In the magnificent chapel of the most reverend archbishop of Toledo, Fonseca of good memory, I saw skillful singers make counterpoint, which if it were written down, would be sold as good composition."[20] It is remarkable how free of errors Chamaterò's counterpoint is (did he make corrections when writing it out?), and we well might ask how one singer avoids singing the same thing as another, and how they know when the tenor has gone below the bass, changing the consonance requirements (in m. 6, for instance, if the quintus singer sees the G in the CF, how will he know he can sing a C above?). However, yielding to clear the way for another part, and indicating with a hand gesture when and how far the tenor singer goes below the CF, were spectacularly illustrated by

---

18. Pietro Pontio, *Ragionamento di musica* (Parma: E. Viotto, 1588; facs. Kassel: Bärenreiter, 1959), III, 89, has a list of features of counterpoint that doesn't mention rests (cf. infra). He allows rests in a counterpoint when satisfying an obligation like canon (III, 91-92), and explicitly allows rests in a duo as distinct from a counterpoint (III, 93).
19. Morley, annotations "Upon the Second part," quoted in Ross Duffin, "*Contrapunctus Simplex et Diminutus*: Polyphonic Improvisation for Voices in the Fifteenth Century," *Basler Jahrbuch für historische Musikpraxis* (2007): 76-77.
20. "En la extremada capilla del reverendíssimo arçobispo de Toledo, Fonseca de buena memoria vi tan diestros cantores echar contrapunto, que si se puntara: se vendiera por buena composición." Juan Bermudo, *Comiença el libro llamado declaración de instrumentos musicales* (Seville: J. de Leòn, 1555; facs. Kassel: Bärenreiter, 1957), ch. 16, fol. cxxviij.

Ensemble le chant sur le livre, directed by Jean-Yves Haymoz, in their evening concert at the Orpheus Academy.[21]

INVERTIBLE COUNTERPOINT

This is discussed explicitly in relation to improvisation by Angleria, Rodio, Brunelli, and Chiodino (who was later translated by Herbst), and Morley includes it in a discussion of descanting.[22] Most treatises show two-part invertible counterpoint exemplified as a florid line added to a CF, suggesting that it was another technique to be used in ex tempore singing. What role might invertible counterpoint have played in liturgical performance, and how might it have been carried out? We find the technique used in a few keyboard examples of psalm and canticle versets.[23] One might apply the same principle in any situation where the CF repeats.

If inversion is done by two singers switching parts, two performance problems arise: 1) the singer of the CF in the original combination must, while singing, listen to and remember what was sung by the contrapuntist so as to be able to repeat it; and 2) both singers must know on what note to start the *replica* (the inverted combination). The second problem can only be solved in advance, with discussion. Specifically, if invertible counterpoint at the twelfth is used, and the original began with the vertical interval of an octave, the *replica* will begin on a fifth. On what

---

21. Ross Duffin posits that when one singer goes below the CF, it is that singer who "controls the direction of the overall counterpoint…" (Ross Duffin, "Contrapunctus Simplex et Diminutus: Polyphonic Improvisation for Voices in the Fifteenth Century," *Basler Jahrbuch für historische Musikpraxis* (2007): 90.), although he does not mention hand gestures as a way of showing the exact interval below the tenor to which the bass singer is about to move, which is crucial to the other singers.

22. See Peter Schubert, "Counterpoint pedagogy in the Renaissance," in *The Cambridge history of Western music theory*, ed. Thomas Christensen (Cambridge: Cambridge University Press, 2002), 514-517 for citations and a discussion.

23. Julie Cumming has suggested, in conversation with the author, the pairs of strophes in hymns. A keyboard example is shown in Peter Schubert, *Modal Counterpoint, Renaissance Style*, 2nd ed. (New York: Oxford University Press, 2008), ex. 13-8a, where each half versicle is sounded twice, once with the counterpoint above the CF, once below.

notes will each singer start, how far will each part be transposed? This problem might have been addressed historically by the tenorist, who might have functioned as the traffic cop for whoever was improvising.[24] At the Orpheus Academy the problem was solved by a discussion beforehand, in which it was agreed that the singer of the CF in the original would sing the improvised line an octave higher in the *replica*, while the singer of the low part would sing the CF a fifth below its original position, i.e., a fourth above his last note. (The CF is a *soggetto cavato* based on the vowels of an Italian dish suggested by a member of the audience: "*rigatoni*" = *mi fa sol mi*, plus a cadence, *fa mi*).

Example 4. Inversion at the twelfth as performed ex tempore by the author and Catherine Motuz[25]

Now that we have seen how *contraponto fugato* and invertible counterpoint might have been improvised, we will look at a composed example that uses both techniques combined, the opening of Pierre de la Rue's Salve II (Example 5a).[26] Here the sopranos could easily have improvised their line against the CF in the tenor. However, for the basses to imitate them (albeit a tone down), invertible counterpoint must be used—in this case invertible at the octave. That means that the soprano line can contain no fifths in metric or melodic positions where consonance is

---

24. Rob C. Wegman has investigated the reasons for the importance of the tenorist in "From Maker to Composer: Improvisation and Musical Authorship in the Low Countries, 1450-1500," *Journal of the American Musicological Society* 49/3 (1996): 444-449.
25. The author is grateful to Joeri Buysse for supplying the recording of the demonstration from which several examples are transcribed.
26. See Petrus de la Rue, *Motetti libro quarto* (Venice: Petrucci, 1505 [=*RISM* 1505²]), item 4, four partbooks (Discantus: ff. 45r-4v; Tenor: ff. 35v-36r; Contratenor: ff. 68r-68v; Bassus: ff. 100r-100v) and Pierre de La Rue, *The Complete Magnificats, Three Salve Reginas*, VivaVoce, dir. Peter Schubert, Naxos 8.557896-97, 2 compact discs (2007).

required (they would invert to fourths). The technique that is to be used for the repetition of the florid line partially determines the melodic content of that line (that is, which consonances can occupy long or metrically strong beats).

The next phrase (*vita dulcedo* beginning in m. 24) is a variant of the first. A new melody is sounded against the CF, first below, then above. Here the bass sings a line that contains a vertical fifth in a strong position. This interval is possible because when the soprano enters it inverts the original combination of m. 24 at the tenth, so the fifth inverts to a sixth as shown in Example 5b.

Example 5a. Pierre de la Rue, Salve II, *mm. 1-5 (note values halved)*

Example 5b. mm. 24-28 (note values halved)

In a general way we can say that whatever interval of invertible counterpoint is used, it will determine which vertical intervals will successfully invert, which will in turn affect the countermelodies sounded against the soggetto. Thus the choice of countermelody depends on the use to which the combination will be put when it is repeated. Or, to look at the problem from the other end, if the composer desperately wanted a melody that created a vertical fifth in the opening duo, he would have had to forgo invertible counterpoint at the octave.

Adding Two Lines in Canon to a CF

This is a task that most of us would have some trouble writing, much less improvising. Vicenzo Lusitano gives patterns for canons above patterned CFs at the fourth, fifth, octave, and unison, at time intervals of minim and semiminim. I laboriously taught myself to do this, but only at one time and one pitch interval: at the minim a fourth above.[27] For the Orpheus Academy I did this same type as a community project, with the audience choosing from among Lusitano's motions shown in Example 6a.[28] That is, given any 2-note CF motion, Lusitano has at least one solution. (Sometimes, when it is impossible to connect, a rest is used.) By memorizing them, the singer is equipped with a *thesaurus* of responses to any CF motion—the adventure is in connecting them. Example 6b shows our "rigatoni" CF and the choices from Lusitano's inventory assembled (and labeled).

---

27. Peter Schubert, "Composing Without a Score ca. 1600" (paper presented at the annual meeting of the Society for Music Theory, Atlanta, GA, November 13, 1999).
28. Vincente [Vincentio, Vencenzo] Lusitano, *Introduttione facilissima, et novissima, di canto fermo, figurato, contraponto semplice, et in concerto* (Venice: A. Baldo, 1553, and F. Rampazetto, 1561; facs. of 1561 ed. Rome: Libreria musicale italiana editrice, 1989). The chart, based on Lusitano, is taken from Peter Schubert, *Modal Counterpoint, Renaissance Style*, 2nd ed. (New York: Oxford University Press, 2008), 319-320. Julian Grimshaw, in "Morley's rule for first-species canon," *Early Music* 34/4 (2006): 661-668, erroneously states that Lusitano "does not set his canonic voices against a tenor" (p. 664).

Example 6a. Lusitano's possibilities, labeled a-m (✓ = three pitch-class sonority)

Example 6b. Canon on the "rigatoni" CF according to Lusitano, using possibilities b, f, c, and h

Zarlino also discusses this technique, first in the 1558 edition of *Le istitutioni harmoniche* and then in a revised and expanded form in 1573 edition (in both editions this discussion is in Book III, chapter 63). In the earlier edition the chapter is only two and a half pages long and contains two examples of canon at the unison and two of canon at the fifth below.[29] In the later edition, the same chapter is fifteen pages long and contains twelve examples of canons at unisons, octaves above, and fifths both above and below.[30] (In addition, the chapter contains examples and a discussion of three-voice stretto fuga, to be discussed below.) The later edition has been discussed by Denis Collins, who summarized Zarlino's rules and reprinted his examples.[31] Here is his new, enthusiastic 1573 rhetoric:

> Of the various kinds of three-voice counterpoint that are made mentally in canon over a cantus firmus, and of some canons that are made from fantasy, and what must be observed in each. Chapter 63.
>
> ...It is thing of no small wonder to see some things arise from the harmonic numbers in music when they are put into action by the musician: which, if one did not hear and see it, one would scarcely be able to believe... how such and such harmonies are to be represented to the hearing, with new and varied shapes, such that it will be staggering to

---

29. Gioseffo Zarlino, *Le istitutioni harmoniche* (Venice: Franceschi, 1558; facs. New York: Broude Bros., 1965), 256-258.
30. Gioseffo Zarlino, *Le istitutioni harmoniche* (Venice: Franceschi Senese, 1573; facs. Ridgewood, NJ: Gregg Press, 1966), 302-317.
31. Denis Collins, "Zarlino and Berardi as Teachers of Canon," *Theoria* 7 (1993): 103-23.

hear; he sings a single part, pulling out from it (so to speak) one or more parts after in consequence. ...The reason I wanted to discuss this matter at length is so that the gentle, virtuous and noble spirits not be deprived of these secrets, not only if they wish to do it mentally, but also (knowing it), that they be able to use it in their compositions, and to find in it by these means endless other inventions.[32]

Where Zarlino had written matter-of-factly about canon against a CF in the 1558 edition, now he waxes positively rhapsodic! I think much of his enthusiasm is aroused by the other element included in the same chapter, stretto fuga.

STRETTO FUGA

It is surely for stretto fuga that Zarlino emphasized improvisation, expanded the rules, added examples, and expressed wonderment. It sounds either as though he heard it for the first time after the 1558 edition, or as though it was a technique largely kept secret by teachers and that he is publicizing their *Secreti* for the first time in a treatise on vocal music.[33] This technique has nothing to do with a long CF fixed in advance; it is, as Zarlino says, "made from fantasy."

---

32. "Delle varie sorti de Contrapunti a Tre voci, che si fanno a mente in Consequenza sopra un Soggetto: & di alcune Consequenze, che si fanno di fantasia, & quello che in ciascheduna si hà de osservare. Capitolo. 63.
E cosa di non poca maraviglia il veder nascere alcune cose nella Musica da i Numeri harmonici; quando dal Musico, il qual sappia conoscere la natura loro, sono posti in atto: che se non udissero & anco vedessero impossibile sarebbe quasi di poterle credere... come si debbere rappresentare al senso dell'Udito tante e tante harmonie, con nuove foggie et varietate; che sarà un stupore di udirle; cantando lui una sola parte, tirandosene (dirò cosi) dietro una, o più in Consequenza. ...Il perche volendo io al presente di queste cose copiosamente ragionare; acciò che li Spiriti gentili, virtuosi & nobili non siano privi di queste Secreti, non solamente volendoli fare a mente; ma acciò che (sapendoli) accommodar etiando li possono nelle loro Compositioni; & ritrovare in esse col loro mezo infinite altre belle inventioni." Zarlino, *Le institutioni harmoniche* (1573), III, ch. 63, 302-303.
33. Busse Berger cites Zacconi on the culture of secrecy (Anna Maria Busse Berger, "The Problem of Diminished Counterpoint," in *Uno gentile et subtile ingenio: Studies in Renaissance Music in Honour of Bonnie J. Blackburn*, ed. Gioa Filocamo and M. Jennifer Bloxam (Turnhout: Brepols, 2009), 24).

I first heard of stretto fuga from John Milsom in 2000 at an Indian restaurant in Montreal (the term is his coinage). He said he thought that Renaissance musicians followed simple rules for conceiving of canons, and told me what they were.[34] I regarded this as a convincing conjecture, but since I had never seen it described in a treatise, I was not eager to use it as a category of compositional process. A year later I found it in the writings of Francisco de Montanos, in two short sentences in the section of his treatise called "on composition."[35] I might not have noticed these sentences were it not for Milsom's having alerted me. He has since found it in Thomas de Sancta Maria and, in a garbled form, in Thomas Morley, and I have found it in Rocco Rodio.[36]

Sancta Maria is probably the first to discuss it, in his treatise on keyboard improvisation. In stretto fuga, the time interval is always one unit of consonance, which Sancta Maria illustrates as both semibreves and minims, referring always to the entrance of the

---

34. Milsom was attending a conference ("Form and Expression in Renaissance Polyphony" at the Faculty of Music, McGill University, February 12-13, 2000), organized by Julie Cumming and the author. Milsom has discussed *stretto fuga* in "'Imitatio,' 'intertextuality', and early music," in *Citation and authority in Medieval and Renaissance musical culture: Learning from the learned*, ed. Suzannah Clark and Elizabeth Eva Leach (Woodbridge: Boydell & Brewer, 2005), 141-51. See also Milsom, "'Josquin and the Combinative Impulse', On the Relationship of Imitation and Text Treatment?," in *The Motet around 1500*, ed. Thomas Schmidt-Beste (Turnhout: Brepols, 2012), 187-222.
35. Francisco de Montanos, *Arte de musica theorica y pratica* (Valladolid: F. de Cordoba, 1592), "de compostura" fols. 9v and 10v.
36. Tomás de Santa María [Thomas de Sancta Maria], *Libro llamado arte de tañer fantasia* (Valladolid: F. Fernandez, 1565; facs. Geneva: Minkoff, 1973), II, ch. 33, "Del modo de hazer fugas," ff. 66v. and 67r.; Thomas Morley, *A Plaine and Easie Introduction to Practicall Musicke* (London: Peter Short, 1597; facs. Oxford: Shakespeare Association, 1937), 98; Rocco Rodio, *Regole di musica*, (Naples: Carlino and Vitale, 1609), pp. 27 and 29. Julian Grimshaw discusses the Morley passage in "Morley's rule for first species canon," *Early Music* 34/4 (2006): 661-666. The technique shows up in earlier treatise examples without discussion. See for instance Johannes Hothby, *De arte contrapuncti*, Ms. Ed. Gilbert Reaney (Neuhausen-Stuttgart: American Institute of Musicology / Hänssler, 1977, CSM v. 26). Ch. 3. Spetie tenore del contrapunto prima. (*GB-Lbl* Add.36986, ff.26–30), 88-91, exx.10-11. "Debbasi qualche volta usare fuga col tinore o col contrapunto, spettando o 2 o piu note, tanto che si senta quasi un simili andaré di note o di voce: exenplo." Folker Froebe cites Hothby's examples of stretto fuga at the fifth and octave in "Satzmodelle," Example 3.

second voice on the *segundo punto* of the first, regardless of the rhythmic value. The earliest stretto fugas are found in 15th-c. canons at the minim, (e.g., in the duo sections of Dufay's "Nuper rosarum flores"), and in later 16th c. repertoire we find it in semibreves and breves. Sancta Maria frames the rule as a prohibition: in making a canon at the fifth above, do not sing the following melodic intervals: 2nd up, 4th up, 3rd down, 5th down.[37] For a canon at the fifth below, the direction of the melodic intervals is reversed.[38] Any melody sung in even values using those melodic intervals and imitated after one value will produce good counterpoint.[39]

Singing a melodic unison (repeating a note) is also possible, but this is not included in his rules, nor in those of Montanos, who repeats Sancta Maria's rules exactly. However, both authors' illustrations in note-against-note semibreves employ the unison as a melodic interval, expanding the melodic possibilities.[40] Montanos follows each first species structure with the same example to which simple embellishments have been added.[41]

Apart from Sancta Maria, Montanos, Morley and Rodio, few authors deal with the subject explicitly. Coclico uses *stretto fuga* at the fifth in seven examples in his treatise: twice to illustrate mode or tone, once to illustrate note-against-note counterpoint, and four times in the section on composition to illustrate imitation

---

37. Santa María, *Arte*, II, ch. 33, f. 66v.
38. Santa María, *Arte*, II, ch. 33, f. 67r.
39. There are some corollary rules that I have developed with experience: not to sing a fifth after another interval in the same direction, nor to sing a fourth after an interval in the same direction, as these will produce similar motion to a perfect interval.
40. Sancta María wants his fugas to be invertible at the octave; a melodic unison would result in the vertical interval of a fifth, which, when inverted at the octave, becomes a fourth. Montanos's fugas are not invertible at the octave.
41. The embellishments include what I call the "double option," which says that if you can go up a fourth or a step, you can do both inside the measure, as long as the next note could have been approached from both. I assume such formulas were also memorized, even if this was never stated explicitly. See Peter Schubert, *Modal Counterpoint, Renaissance Style*, 2nd ed. (New York: Oxford University Press, 2008), 156-159; and Peter Schubert, "Counterpoint pedagogy in the Renaissance," in *The Cambridge history of Western music theory*, ed. Thomas Christensen (Cambridge: Cambridge University Press, 2002), 518. Sancta Maria gives rules for fugas at the octave, and examples of canons at the fourth and fifth after two notes.

and music in more parts.⁴² Elsewhere, Zarlino says "But the too continual [use of] such closeness [of imitation] causes it to have fallen into a certain common way of composing, such that nowadays a fuga is not to be found that has not been used thousands and thousands of times by various composers."⁴³ I used to think this was rhetorical exaggeration, but if he is talking about stretto fuga at the fifth, it's almost an understatement: since from any note we have only five possible notes to go to next, we can calculate that there are only 625 different five-note melodies possible!

Three-voice stretto fuga is discussed by Sancta Maria and Zarlino. Sancta Maria illustrates only one way, in which the second voice follows an octave below the first after one *compas* (semibreve) and the third enters a fourth below the first after 2 *compases*.⁴⁴ The list of prohibited intervals is the same as for two-part stretto fuga at the fifth above (because the third voice follows the second a fifth above), with the additional proscription of the melodic descending step. This is because the combination made by the first and second voices is inverted at the twelfth when it recurs between the second and third voices, and a melodic step produces a vertical sixth, which will invert to a seventh. This is shown in Example 7a, where the melodic motion of a second in the alto produces a vertical sixth, which inverts to a seventh between the soprano and bass. The beginning of Sancta Maria's fully embellished example is shown in Example 7b.⁴⁵

---

42. These are exx. 11, 15, 53, 70, 73, 74, and 76 in Seay's translation (see note 1). Ex. 53 breaks off the canon after eight notes; in ex. 70 the use of *stretto fuga* is intermittent; ex. 73 is a "stacked" 3-vv. canon; ex. 74 is a 3-vv. invertible canon; and ex. 76 is a pair of imitative duos. For more on these types, see Peter Schubert, "Hidden Forms in Palestrina's *First Book of Four-Voice Motets*," *Journal of the American Musicological Society* 60/3 (2007): 500-504.
43. "Ma il troppo continouare cotal vicinità fece, che si cascò in un certo modo commune di comporre, che al presente non si ritrova quasi Fuga, che non sia stata usata mille migliata di volte da diversi Compositori." Zarlino, *Institutioni harmoniche* (1558), III, ch. 51, 213.
44. Tomás de Santa María [Thomas de Sancta Maria], *Libro llamado arte de tañer fantasia* (Valladolid: F. Fernandez, 1565; facs. Geneva: Minkoff, 1973), II, ch. 33, f. 68r.
45. The fact that it contains so many sequences may be a sign that sequences are more appropriate to instrumental music; I have mentioned the possibility that sequence is more appropriate to instrumental music in Peter Schubert, "A Lesson from Lassus: Form in the Duos of 1577," *Music Theory Spectrum* 17/1 (1995): 1-26.

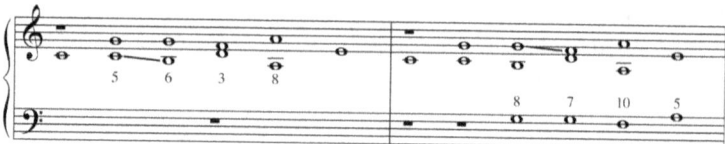

Example 7a. Melodic seconds work in two voices but not in three.

Example 7b. Sancta Maria's three-voice stretto fuga, beginning

Zarlino treats both adding two voices in canon to a CF and three-voice stretto fuga in the same chapter of the second edition of the *Istitutioni* (1573). After giving examples of two parts added in canon to a CF, Zarlino wants "to show some kinds of double consequences that are made mentally without a subject [i.e., not against a CF]."[46] He gives three examples; the first is at the fifth below and the octave above the first voice at a time interval of four semibreves; the second is of the same type, but is a stretto fuga after one semibreve; the third is also a stretto fuga at the octave below and the fifth above the first voice, also after a semibreve. Rather than give lists of prohibited melodic intervals, he simply says not to make vertical sixths (see Example 7a).

In fact, there are four ways to make three-voice stretto fuga, employing different combinations of imitation. The three voices may enter in the order HLM (high-low-middle) or LHM, or MLH, or MHL, with the outer parts an octave apart and the middle part a fifth from the immediately previous one.[47] Reconstructions of three improvisations at the Orpheus Academy are shown in Example 8.

a)

---

46. Gioseffo Zarlino, *Le institutioni harmoniche* (Venice: Franceschi, 1558; facs. New York: Broude Bros., 1965), III, ch. 63, 314. The beginnings of two *stretto fugas* are transcribed in Denis Collins, "Zarlino and Berardi as Teachers of Canon," *Theoria* 7 (1993): 118-119. They demonstrate the guide voice skipping on the weak half note (the "double option").

47. The four possibilities, albeit with longer time intervals of imitation, are discussed and schematized in Peter Schubert, *Modal Counterpoint, Renaissance Style*, 2nd ed. (New York: Oxford University Press, 2008), ch. 16.

Example 8a-c. Three-voice stretto fugas improvised by Catherine Motuz, Steven VandeMoortele, and the author[48]

These examples, albeit rudimentary, sound like Renaissance music, and they are especially satisfying in that each one contains full sonorities containing a third and a fifth. They exemplify modal problems that improvisers must have dealt with: first, that one may begin by accident in a transposed mode, and second, that fuga at the fifth above (Example 8a & c) might tend to wander sharpward while fuga at the fifth below (Example 8b) might wander flatward.

Stretto fuga has been noticed by scholars looking at repertoire and later treatises: Gregory Butler sees it as the very meaning

---

48. More demonstrations of improvised canons are available on YouTube at the following addresses:
http://www.youtube.com/watch?v=no1J393WpKk
http://www.youtube.com/watch?v=nxJa9YDP3MU
http://www.youtube.com/watch?v=eu_-OfAABHw
http://www.youtube.com/watch?v=w664qFsO9gg

of the word "fantasy" and traces it back to the "Fantasies de Joskin," continuing with examples from Sermisy and Zarlino through to the 18th c.[49] Michael R. Dodds has tracked sequential patterns (which occur in many stretto fugas) from Lusitano to Werckmeister.[50] And Robert Gauldin has formalized stretto fuga mathematically (Gauldin is the only author to try to explain canon at longer time intervals).[51]

Once we are fully aware these formulas, we see that they abound in repertoire. One example comes from Jessie Ann Owens' chapter on Isaac. Writing about Isaac's skill at turning chant into polyphony, she writes:

> Given the importance of the chant, it might seem reasonable to assume that Isaac began by composing the entire line that would bear the chant and then added the other voices. However, the physical evidence of the writing on the bifolio, as well as the music itself, suggests otherwise. It appears that he composed the piece one section at a time. ... Within each section, Isaac worked phrase by phrase, point by point. He had a number of different options for creating each point. One approach was to deploy the chant in two voices as a kind of frame. He did this in two ways. In one, either the discantus imitates the altus a fourth higher at the distance of a semibreve or a breve (phrases 1, 2, 3, 7, and 8), or the tenor imitates the discantus an octave lower at the distance of a breve (phrases 5 and 15).[52]

The phrase "two voices as a kind of frame" in several cases means arranging the chant into stretto fuga. In verse 1 the full-textured opening hides this technique; the soprano actually begins the fuga a semibreve later, as bracketed in Ex. 9.

---

49. Gregory G. Butler, "The Fantasia as Musical Image," *Musical Quarterly* 60/4 (1974): pp. 602-615; William Porter, "Reconstructing 17th-century North German improvisational practice," *GOArt Research Reports* 2 (2000): 25-39.
50. Michael R. Dodds, "Columbus's Egg: Andreas Werckmeister's Teachings on Contrapuntal Improvisation in *Harmonologia musica* (1702)," *Journal of Seventeenth-Century Music* 12/1 (2006), http://www.sscm-jscm.org/v12/no1/dodds.html.
51. Robert Gauldin, "The Composition of Late Renaissance Stretto Canons," *Theory and Practice* 21 (1996): 29-54.
52. Jessie Ann Owens, *Composers at Work: The Craft of Musical Composition 1450-1600* (New York: Oxford University Press, 1997), 268-269.

Example 9. Isaac, phrase 1 (after Owens; the first breve in the discantus has been broken into two semibreves to show the stretto fuga between the two upper parts; the dotted line connects the guide in the alto with the consequent in the discantus)

Phrases 3 and 7 likewise work this way, also in canon at the fourth above. We can easily imagine that Isaac inspected the chant and saw immediately that its motions would accommodate a canon at the fourth above. The melodic motions of up a step, down a step, and down a third govern the line for the first nine semibreves. However, one cannot go down more than one step at a time in canon at the fourth above (parallel fifths would result), so Isaac speeds up the seventh and ninth notes as passing semiminims, making a chain of descending thirds on principal metric positions. In fact, any chant can be made into stretto fuga if properly rhythmicized.⁵³ In the Isaac example, the melodic content of the chant partially determined the *inventio* that governs each point of imitation (see n. 8).

Example 10. The original chant (after Owens)

This brief survey of some improvisatory techniques might make us wonder how composition differs from improvisation, where improvisation ends and composition begins. In the following section I will look at three treatises whose authors use the word "composition" and make some distinctions between that and improvisation. Unfortunately, the three authors do not always make the distinctions in the same places!

---

53. In "Chant Paraphrase Canon: Straitjacket or Instinctive Behaviour?," a paper presented at the Medieval and Renaissance Music Conference, Barcelona, Spain, 6 July 2011, the author and Julie Cumming demonstrated extemporaneously making a stretto fuga out of a chant melody.

2.
COMPOSITION

When he had seen his students firmly grounded in singing, able to pronounce neatly, to sing ornately and to put the text in the correct place, he taught them the perfect and imperfect types (of consonances) and the way of singing counterpoint on plainchant with these types. Those whom he noticed to be of high ability and happy soul he taught in a few words the rule of composing for three voices, afterwards for four, five, six, etc., always providing examples for them to imitate.[54] ... The first requirement of a good composer is that he should know how to sing counterpoint by improvisation. Without this he will be nothing (Coclico).[55]

You should know (as I have said) that from this florid, or diminished, counterpoint come a variety of compositions, like masses, motets, psalms, ricercars, lamentations, and madrigals (Pontio).[56]

... singing extempore upon a plainsong is indeede a peece of cunning, and very necessarie to be perfectly practiced of him who meaneth to be a composer for bringing of a quick sight, yet is it a great absurditie so to seek for a sight, as to make it the end of our studie... (Morley).[57]

Before beginning to untangle the difference between counterpoint and composition, it must be admitted that not all authors make a clear distinction. Ferand noted Vicentino's use of the

---

54. Adrianus Petit Coclico, *Compendium musices* (Nuremberg: Montanus and Neuber, 1552; facs. Kassel: Bärenreiter, 1954), trans. Albert Seay as *Musical Compendium* (Colorado Springs: Colorado College Music Press, 1973), 16.
55. "Primum itaque quod in bono compositore desideratur, est, ut contrapunctum ex tempore canere sciat" (Coclico, *Compendium*, sig. L ii, verso). Seay's translation has "singer" for "composer" (p. 24), which is quite misleading.
56. "Voi dovete sapere (come già vi dissi) che da questo contrapunto florido, over deminuito vengano variate compositioni, come Messe, Motetti, Salmi, Recercari, Lamentationi, & Madrigali." Pietro Pontio, *Ragionamento di musica* (Parma: E. Viotto, 1588; facs. Kassel: Bärenreiter, 1959), IV, 123; see also pp. 21 and 153.
57. Thomas Morley, *A Plaine and Easie Introduction to Practicall Musicke* (London: Peter Short, 1597; facs. Oxford: Shakespeare Association, 1937), 215.

phrase "composing in the mind,"[58] and Zarlino dodges the question entirely. Bermudo, on the other hand, says: "There is the art of counterpoint, and that of composition. These terms differ in that composition is a collection and joining of many discrete parts with distinct harmony, particular concordances and special fine devices. Counterpoint is an improvised arrangement on a plainsong with varied melodies."[59]

Our three authors agree that counterpoint is prior to composition (that is, the voice-leading rules are mostly the same), and they agree that counterpoint is essential to composition. Morley and Bermudo decry those who know no counterpoint and yet would try to compose.[60] But composition is not merely written-down improvisation, it must involve other considerations; but which? The areas that our three authors seem to agree on can be grouped into the following categories:

1. *Mode.* An improviser does not have to concern himself much with mode when working with a CF, so mode is more often included as a feature of composition when the distinction is

---

58. Nicola Vicentino, *L'antica música ridotta alla moderna prattica* (Rome, A. Barre, 1555; facs. Kassel: Bärenreiter, 1959), Book IV, ch. 23 is titled "Modo di comporre alla mente sopra i canti fermi." See Ernst Ferand, *Die Improvisation in der Musik* (Zurich: Rhein-Verlag, 1938), 204.
59. "Ay arte de contrapunto, y de composicion. Differen estos dos nombres en alguna manera, que a la composicion llaman colección, o ayuntamiento de muchas partes discretas, y distintas de harmonia, con particulares concordancias, y especiales primores. El contrapunto es una ordenación improvisa sobre canto llano, con diversas melodías" (Juan Bermudo, *Comiença el libro llamado declaración de instrumentos musicales* (Seville: J. de Leòn, 1555; facs. Kassel: Bärenreiter, 1957), ch. 16, fol. cxxviij r.).
60. Morley: "...although it be unpossible for them to compose without it [counterpoint], but they rather employ their time in making of songes, which remain for the posterity then to sing descant which is no longer known then the singers mouth is open expressing it, and for the most part cannot be twise repeated in one manner" (*Plaine and Easie*, 121). Bermudo offers those who don't know counterpoint an aid in the form of writing in score with barlines through the system of three staves. This suggests that knowing counterpoint entailed reading parts printed separately on one or more pages. "Algunos que no saben contrapunto, y quieren començar a componer con sola cuenta de consonancias suelen virgular el papel pantado por no perderse en la cuenta. Y aunque este modo sea barbaro: porne exemplo del para los que tuvieren necessidad, y quisieren seguirlo" (*Declaración*, ch. 27, fol. cxxxiiij r.).

made at all.⁶¹ (However, I have found that some knowledge of mode is essential when improvising three-voice *stretto fuga*, as I have often ended up in untenable *ficta* situations!)

2. *Text.* Many of the ways that text influences musical setting (speed, mode, interval affect, word-painting, cadence) might be ignored in improvisation, but are discussed in connection with composition. As for prosody, if improvisers sang words at all (as in Banchieri's Example 2), minimal attention to correct prosody would probably suffice, and so prosody is not an issue in discussions of improvisation.

3. *Vertical sonority.* This category includes spacing and chord content. Most improvised counterpoint is in two parts, with the range of the parts presumably depending on the improvisers' voice ranges. In three-part improvised techniques, the ranges of the parts is never an issue: sometimes it falls naturally out of the technique itself, as in fauxbourdon, parallel-sixth and -tenth models, and stretto fuga as described by Zarlino, where the ranges are in alternating authentic and plagal modes.⁶² However, composition brings with it the problem of managing more parts in several different ranges, which explains why theorists print tables of consonant sonorities and discuss *voci pari* texture. As for pitch content, Pontio (like Zarlino) specifies that three-voice sonorities should contain a fifth and a third.

---

61. This inference, based on my three treatises, is flatly contradicted by Lusitano (see Philippe Canguilhem, "Singing upon the book according to Vicente Lusitano," *Early Music History* 30 (2011): 55-103. 81). Lusitano's views on the difference between counterpoint and composition are summarized in Canguilhem "Singing upon the book," 95-97. Another exception to my inference might include Ramis's discussion of mode in a note-against-note context. See Bartolomeus Ramis de Pareia, *Musica practica* (Bologna: B. de Hiriberia, 1482; facs. Bologna: Forni, 1969), ed. Johannes Wolf as *Musica practica Bartolomei Rami de Pareja Bononiae* (Leipzig: Breitkopf und Härtel, 1901), part II, tract 1, ch. 2, 72. This passage is discussed in Peter Schubert, "Counterpoint pedagogy in the Renaissance," in *The Cambridge history of Western music theory*, ed. Thomas Christensen (Cambridge: Cambridge University Press, 2002), 508-9.

62. That is, the outer voices are an octave apart, and the middle part is a fifth from one of them. Zarlino writes that if one part is in the authentic, the adjacent part(s) should be in the plagal mode (*Le istitutioni harmoniche* 1558, IV, ch. 31, 338). In Banchieri's Ex. 2 the voices are unusually far apart, as they are in some of Lusitano's examples (see n. 7).

4. *Cadences.* Improvisers knew how to make 2-voice cadences with suspensions. Although I have never seen a discussion of making cadences in *stretto fuga*, one can easily invent formulas for them. But on which notes to cadence, and making cadences in more parts, these are a problem—for these, theorists supplied model cadences (commonplaces) in four to six parts.[63]
5. *Choosing good models.* References to specific composers and pieces is generally reserved for parts of treatises dealing with composition.[64]
6. *Awareness of genre and style.* An improviser need not apparently concern himself with musically differentiating a madrigal from a motet, but a composer must. And eschewing passé fashion, as Morley urged, might not be an issue for an improviser.

Coclico

The frontispiece of Coclico's treatise lists three subjects: singing ornately; the rules of counterpoint; and composition. This division is not reflected in the book, however, which is in only two parts. The first treats the hexachord, mutation, and tones of the psalms; the second treats both counterpoint and composition.

Coclico lists seven requirements for a good composer:
1. the ability to sing counterpoint ex tempore
2. strong desire
3. knowledge of the use of intervals
4. awareness of mode
5. knowledge of mensuration signs
6. care to match text affect with mode, and prosody with rhythm
7. use of imitation between parts

---

63. Peter Schubert, "Musical Commonplaces in the Renaissance," in *Music Education in the Middle Ages and Renaissance*, ed. Russell E. Murray, Susan Forscher Weiss, and Cynthia J. Cyrus (Bloomington: Indiana University Press, 2010), 161-192.
64. See Howard Mayer Brown, "Emulation, Competition, and Homage: Imitation and Theories of Imitation in the Renaissance," *Journal of the American Musicological Society* 35/1 (1982): 1-48.

Regarding the first two, we have seen the quotes in the epigraph to this part. The third goes beyond the use of vertical intervals in improvisation, which only applied in two parts; here Coclico is dealing with three and more parts, so he shows the legal use of the fourth and offers comments and examples of chord voicing and vocal ranges. Regarding the fourth requirement, awareness of mode, he mentions regular and irregular, and warns against a line exceeding its limits and wandering about. He uses the term "tone," which must be contrasted with the psalm tones described in the first part of his book: a chorister improvising would need to know how antiphons connect to the Doxology, but would not need to know the ranges of the modes and the species of fourth and fifth. The fifth and sixth requirements speak for themselves. In connection with the seventh and last requirement, the use of imitation (which he regards as a recent invention), he gives examples in two to seven voices. There he suggests emulating the most learned musicians in various countries ("....*in Italia Gallia, & Flandria eruditissimi Musici*").[65]

PONTIO

The four *ragionamenti* (discussions, dialogues) of Pontio's 1588 treatise are not given titles, and although references are made to composition and counterpoint throughout, it is the fourth *ragionamento* that most clearly addresses composition, while the second and third are more focused on counterpoint. At the beginning of the second *ragionamento*, Pontio distinguishes between *contrapunto* and *compositione*. He says the former is a step on the way to the latter.[66] He organizes this *ragionamento* as a list of the various contexts in which each vertical interval can be used (like

---

65. Adrianus Petit Coclico, *Compendium musices* (Nuremberg: Montanus and Neuber, 1552; facs. Kassel: Bärenreiter, 1954), trans. Albert Seay as *Musical Compendium* (Colorado Springs: Colorado College Music Press, 1973), sig. M iiii v.
66. "Con questo contrapunto ve ne passate alla compositione." Pietro Pontio, *Ragionamento di musica* (Parma: E. Viotto, 1588; facs. Kassel: Bärenreiter, 1959), II, 21.

Tinctoris[67]). For each interval in a given context, Pontio indicates which motions are appropriate to counterpoint, which to composition, and which to both. Addressing both contrapuntists and composers (or contrapuntists who will eventually be composers), he often mentions specific repertoire examples by well-known composers. Thus in discussing the motion of a unison to a sixth, he says, "One can also go from a unison to a sixth, making the parts move as here [Ex. 11a], which Jachet did in *Messa sine nomine* with the bass and the tenor [Ex. 11b], at the words '*consubstantialem Patri.*' And this passage is more used in compositions of five and six voices than in two-part counterpoint or trios."[68]

Example 11a. (Pontio)

---

67. Johannes Tinctoris, *Liber de arte contrapuncti proportionale musices complexus effectum musices* (1477), ed. Albert Seay, *Corpus Scriptorum de Musica* 22/2 (American Institute of Musicology, 1975), 5-157, trans. Albert Seay as *The Art of Counterpoint*, *Musicological Studies and Documents* 5 (American Institute of Musicology, 1961).

68. "Si potra anco passare dall'Vnisono alla Sesta, facendosi movendo le parti, come qui. Il che fece Iachet nella Messa sine nomine col basso, & col Tenore, sotto queste parole, *Consubstantialem Patri*. Et questo passaggio serve piu alle compositioni di quatro, & cinque voci, ch'al contraponto di due voci, & terzetti" (Pontio, *Ragionamento*, II, p. 30). It is amazing that Pontio had examples of such apparently trivial details of voice-leading at his disposal; memorizing specific interval progressions à la Tinctoris is a significant aspect of improvisation, and having examples at the ready is like having a concordance in one's head. It recalls Cristle Collins Judd's interpretation of Aron's example-gathering in "Reading Aron Reading Petrucci: The Music Examples of the 'Trattato della natura et cognitione di tutti gli tuoni (1525),'" *Early Music History* 14 (1995): 121-152.

Example 11b. (Jachet, Missa Quarti toni sine nomine, Credo *mm. 41-42, note values halved)*[69]

Examples like this straddle the boundary between counterpoint and composition: the particular voice-leading formula is useful to the improviser, but the example links it to a good model and brings awareness of larger contexts.

At the beginning of the third *Ragionamento,* Pontio gives the six requirements for making a counterpoint against a plainsong.[70] They are:

1. conjunct motion
2. long fast scale passages (*belle tirate*)
3. repetition of motives (*replica d'inventione*)
4. no large unsingable intervals (the minor sixth ascending is permitted)
5. few cadences (except to provide a little rest before a new or repeated *inventione*)
6. few octaves or unisons on downbeats

---

69. Jachet of Mantua, *Missa Quarti toni sine nomine* (Venice, 1561), ed. Philip T. Jackson in *Opera Omnia,* vol. 3 (American Institute of Musicology, 1976), 87.
70. Pontio, *Ragionamento,* III, 89-93.

He then defines three types of counterpoint: "diminished," "legato," and "fugato." The principal requirement for diminished counterpoint is the avoidance of long notes on the downbeat (breve, semibreve, or dotted minim), which is appropriate to composition of duos, trios, etc. Legato counterpoint entails the use of semibreves and dotted minims on the weak beats (overlapping the semibreve beat). Fugato involves the repetition of a *passagio*. This type is also called *obligato* or *capriccioso*, and *obligato* includes two lines in canon against a CF. He allows that this technique could be appropriate to composition.

The third *ragionamento* details the differences between a *duo* and counterpoint. The duo occupies an interesting position somewhere in between composition and counterpoint. In a duo one can use the semibreve and dotted minim on the downbeat, one can use cadences and rests, and one is limited to the interval of a thirteenth between the two parts.[71] His example shows a duo with both voices in mixed values. The reason this is a grey area is that an improviser could sing on a figurated (rhythmically varied) CF, like a chanson tune, or a composer could compose a duo.[72] The rest of the third *ragionamento* is about mode and tone. This section is framed more in relation to composers than to *contrapuntisti*, although cadences are permitted in counterpoint, and cadences are an important aspect of mode.[73] Repertoire examples are also cited in his discussion of each mode.[74]

In the fourth *ragionamento* Pontio covers mensuration, and finally lists the five qualities of composition. They are:
1. that it be formed on a mode or tone;
2. that it be formed of consonances and dissonances;
3. that it respect the ends of text phrases (with cadences);
4. that new *inventioni* be found in it (see n. 8); and

---

71. Pontio, *Ragionamento*, III, 93-94.
72. Banchieri recommends that the "new contrapuntist" take a line from an existing piece (he excerpts soprano lines from a sestina by Lasso and pieces by Gesualdo, Monteverdi, Viadana, and Leoni) and invent a new counterpoint to it. See Adriano Banchieri, *Cartella musicale* (Venice: G. Vincenti, 1614; facs. Bologna: Forni, 1983), 161-210.
73. Pontio, *Ragionamento*, III, 94-99.
74. Pontio, *Ragionamento*, III, 99-121.

5. that there always be a third and a fifth when four voices are singing.

There follow various random observations meant only for composers, many of which are explicitly said to be useful to contrapuntists as well. These include: that the distance between the outer voices be limited to a total range of a nineteenth;[75] that imitations be made on the fifth and final of the mode;[76] that the composition end on the final of the mode and that the *soggetto* be appropriate to the mode;[77] and that the mode be appropriate to the words.[78]

Morley

A Plaine and Easie Introduction to Practicall Musicke (1597) is divided into three parts, as stated on the title page: "The first teacheth to sing... The second treateth of descante... The third and last part entreateth of composition..." "Descante" consists of various improvised techniques like those surveyed above: singing in note-against-note counterpoint,(72-78), imitating the CF (p. 76), diminished counterpoint (81-92), singing cadences (82-3), and singing a repeated motive against a CF (to "maintaine a point," – p. 84), singing the inversion of a motive (to "revert a point"—p. 85), adding a third part to an already improvised duo (pp. 92-96), singing two-part canon against a CF (pp. 98-105 – he runs through all intervals of imitation like Cerreto[79]), and singing in invertible counterpoint (pp. 105-115). In his discussion of invertible counterpoint (Morley calls it "double descant"), he says it is "no other thing, but a certain kind of composition, which beeing sung after divers sortes, by changing the partes, maketh divers manners of harmonie."[80] Calling it a type of "composition" while including it

---

75. Pontio, *Ragionamento*, IV, 144.
76. Pontio, *Ragionamento*, IV, 145.
77. Pontio, *Ragionamento*, IV, 146.
78. Pontio, *Ragionamento*, IV, 148
79. Scipone Cerreto, *Della prattica musica vocale et strumentale* (Naples: Iacomo Carlino, 1601; facs. Bologna: Forni, n.d.), III, ch. 16, 228-232.
80. Morley, *Plaine and Easie*, 105

in the book on descant (it is "sung" in the same sentence), Morley seems to equivocate on the place of double counterpoint.

Morley's five examples of double counterpoint are quite different from those of most authors, who show a CF changing positions with the added part. In his first example, showing invertible counterpoint at the twelfth, both voices are figurated (rhythmically mixed), and bits of stretto fuga occur. The examples of invertible counterpoint at the tenth begin with imitation after three semibreves, but then beaks off. His first example of mirror inversion, however, is a figurated line against a CF in semibreves.[81]

His comments on matters specific to composition can be summed up as follows:

1. *Mode*. The problem of cadencing on the wrong note of the mode ("out of the key") is very briefly addressed on pp. 147-148. Later on (p. 156), an example is considered faulty because one of the voices enters on a note that is not proper to the mode. Morley's handling of this issue is perfunctory (he shows examples of falsobordoni in each of the eight psalm tones), and so in the "Annotations upon the third part" he adds a discussion of the traditional eight modes and Glarean's twelve modes.

2. *Text*. Morley begins "Rules to be observed in dittying" with the usual vague exhortation: "...if you have a grave matter, applie a grave kinde of musicke to it" (p. 177). However, in the subsequent discussion he specifies the role of intervals, accidentals, speed of note values, word-painting, correct prosody, avoiding rests in the middle of a word (he is scandalized by an example from Dunstaple) unless expressing the word "sigh," and finally, not using cadences "till the full sence of the words be perfect" (pp. 177-78).

3. *Sonority, spacing, and cadences*. The discussion turns to composition proper (called "setting") with tables of three-voice sonorities and examples of three-voice cadences (pp. 126-128),

---

81. Mirror inversion involves melodic inversion and switching the positions of parts so that the vertical interval sucession is maintained. See Peter Schubert, *Modal Counterpoint, Renaissance Style*, 2nd ed. (New York: Oxford University Press, 2008), 297-98.

followed by tables of four-voice sonorities and many examples of cadences in four to six voices (pp. 129-142). Spacing is again discussed in connection to specific examples (pp. 158 and 163), and later overall ranges (high versus low clefs) are treated, along with *voci pari* voice arrangements (pp. 165-56).

4. *Authority and style*. The third part of the treatise begins with a fairly long (pp. 116-126) review of descant. Two of the examples discussed here (by Pygott and Rysbie, p. 122) are considered too old-fashioned, raising issues of historical awareness and authority. This discussion is in the third part because modeling, imitation and emulation are features of composition, not counterpoint. Later on in this part Morley identifies specific composers and, quoting Zarlino, urges his pupils to choose the best models. He even shows how he would update the music of Taverner (pp. 150-154).

5. *Awareness of genre*. Morley mentions the difference between motet and madrigal a few times (p. 150, p. p. 170-71, and 179), and later he gives fairly detailed descriptions of many other genres (pp. 179-182).

Other matters that fall into the discussion of composition include the need for diversity and descriptions of fancy canonic techniques. Morley commends the Italians for not lingering too long on one "point" (i.e., soggetto, p. 162) and later urges the student to begin with two different soggetti or with one soggetto and its inversion (p. 167). While simple stretto fuga was included in the section on descant, Morley gives many complex examples of canon (pp. 172-176) in the section on composition.

3.
CONCLUSION

Although the term "counterpoint" refers to improvisation (and sometimes only to note-against-note counterpoint), it comprises not only basic voice-leading rules but also sophisticated structural patterns of repetition that will be used in composition. These patterns include adding parts to a CF (in parallel sixths and thirds, with repetition of a motive, with repetition using invertible counterpoint, and with canonic repetition in the added voices) and free canons in 2-4 voices. For us, knowing which techniques could be improvised provides a list of contrapuntal behaviors that we can learn to spot, and that enrich our understanding and appreciation of composed repertoire.[82] Actually trying out what is described in treatises gives us insight into "thinking musically" in the Renaissance. I have found for instance that memory and visualization are essential to success in improvisation, and I feel sure these skills would facilitate composition, especially when composing in sections on erasable *cartelle*. A physical, intuitive understanding of improvisation reveals patterns of thought that lie behind the making of music. Further, it causes us to re-evaluate the esteem (or contempt) in which we hold "learned" the contrapuntal techniques of the day: if a boy could do invertible counterpoint in his head then, when we find it in a composition, it seems not so much "learned" as perfectly natural.

The improviser is actively engaged, responding on the spot, and coming up with little (mostly 2- and 3-voice) combinations, or *inventioni*, that can be used in a composition. The composer has a thesaurus of these the back of his mind, inculcated with his earliest training as a singer. However, to make a finished composition, he has to stand outside and consider various options for the work as a whole. The *inventioni* must deployed in the process

---

82. Julie Cumming has inventoried improvised techniques in several compositions in "From Two-Part Framework to Movable Module," in *Medieval Music in Practice: Essays in Honor of Richard Crocker*, ed. Judith Peraino (Münster: American Institute of Musicology, 2012), 175-214.

of *dispositio* according to artistically self-conscious considerations that are proper to making full-textured pieces of lasting value, pieces that must hold up against masterworks of preceding generations. For this, the composer must find suitable soggetti and an appropriate mode for the text, must articulate a larger structure with cadences, must arrange good-sounding sonorities in many voices, must compose music appropriate to the genre, and must improve on good models. Having improvised as a boy won't help him with these tasks.[83] But, once he has made those choices, the working out of the duos and trios and all the details of counterpoint and voice leading will be a piece of cake.

Treatises may differ on the exact boundary between improvisation and composition, but our three authors clearly believed there was such a boundary, and our understanding of compositional process in the Renaissance must take this into account. Julie Cumming has eloquently expressed several ways that knowledge of improvisatory practice can affect musicology.[84] Our familiarity with those techniques that could be improvised and our ability to distinguish them from those aspects of the piece that were the product of reflection will give us a better "feel" for the music, give depth and precision to our analyses, and make us better able to appreciate the composer's art.

---

83. Our three authors do not talk about duos and trios as building-blocks, but it is covered fairly thoroughly by Montanos, Sancta Maria, and Cerone, whose contributions are discussed in Peter Schubert, "Musical Commonplaces in the Renaissance," in *Music Education in the Middle Ages and Renaissance*, ed. Russell E. Murray, Susan Forscher Weiss, and Cynthia J. Cyrus (Bloomington: Indiana University Press, 2010), 161-192; and in Peter Schubert, "Counterpoint pedagogy in the Renaissance," in *The Cambridge history of Western music theory*, ed. Thomas Christensen (Cambridge: Cambridge University Press, 2002), 519-525.

84. Cumming, Julie E. "Renaissance Improvisation and Musicology," *Music Theory Online* 19/2 (2013), www.mtosmt.org/issues/mto.13.19.2/mto.13.19.2.cumming.php.

PERSONALIA

ROB C. WEGMAN

Rob C. Wegman is an Associate Professor of Music at Princeton University. He specializes in European music broadly from the period 1150–1550. He is the author of two books, *Born for the Muses: The Life and Masses of Jacob Obrecht* (Oxford 1994), and *The Crisis of Music in Early Modern Europe, 1470–1530* (New York, 2005), and has published extensively on musical culture and society in the fifteenth century. His current focus is on thirteenth-century polyphony, particularly the composition and transmission of *organum purum*, the early history of rhythmic notation, and the palaeography and international circulation of musical sources.

JOHANNES MENKE

Johannes Menke studied music education, oboe, music theory, composition, as well as German language and literature in Freiburg im Breisgau. In 2004 he completed his doctoral dissertation on Giacinto Scelsi at the Technische Universität Berlin. From 1999-2009 he taught at the Musikhochschule Freiburg and since 2007, he has been teaching historical composition and theory at the Schola Cantorum Basiliensis. He has also been active as an oboe player, singer and composer. He is editor of the book series *Praxis und Theorie des Partimentospiels*, co-editor of the book series *sinefonia* and a collaborator for the journal *Musik & Ästhetik*. From 2008-2012 he was president of the German-speaking society for music theory.

PETER SCHUBERT

Peter Schubert studied theory and conducting with Nadia Boulanger in Paris and holds a Ph.D. in musicology from Columbia University, where he conducted the Barnard-Columbia Chorus, Opera Uptown, and the New Calliope Singers. Currently an Associate Professor at the McGill University Faculty of Music, Schubert is the author of a groundbreaking and highly regarded textbook, *Modal Counterpoint, Renaissance Style* (Oxford University Press, 1999). In Montreal he founded VivaVoce, which has released four CDs of Renaissance, Romantic, and modern music. He has been invited to give lectures and workshops in the United States, Belgium, Canada, France, Italy, Switzerland and the Netherlands.

FINAL EDITOR
Dirk Moelants

COPY EDITOR
Kathleen Snyers

SERIES EDITOR
Peter Dejans

AUTHORS
Rob C. Wegman
Johannes Menke
Peter Schubert

LAY-OUT
Jurgen Leemans
designed by Filiep Tacq

ISBN 978 90 5867 997 0
D/2014/1869/59
NUR 663

© 2014 by Leuven University Press /
Universitaire Pers Leuven / Presses Universitaires de Louvain
Minderbroedersstraat 4, B-3000 Leuven (Belgium)

All rights reserved.
Except in those cases expressly determined by law,
no part of this publication may be multiplied,
saved in automated data file or made public in any way whatsoever
without the express prior written consent of the publishers.

www.ingramcontent.com/pod-product-compliance
Lightning Source LLC
Chambersburg PA
CBHW052051300426
44117CB00012B/2076